the
VEGETARIAN
kitchen

This is for my family – my wonderful husband Lorne, darling,
beloved Rayne, and of course Gelyn, who has yet
to experience the delights of good food – welcome to the world,
little one, what a fabulous adventure awaits!

MELLISSA BUSHBY

Acknowledgements

I would like to acknowledge the following people, for their invaluable support and patience: My much-loved and inspiring boys, Lorne and Rayne, for their constant advice, inspiration, encouragement and – where necessary – (constructive) criticism; my mother and father, for enabling me to discover my great love for all things bookish; and friends, near and far. The editorial team at Random House Struik, specifically Bev, for fabulous art direction and making my rustic, home recipes look glamorous and gorgeous; Linda, for seeing something there in the first place, and Bronwen, for being so patient with me. Also, the many great vegetarians of the world, who have so motivated me, and thus played no small role in the creation of this book.

The late, great and splendid Luciano Pavarotti said 'One of the very best things about life is how we must regularly stop what we are doing and devote our attention to eating'. Surely, no truer words have ever been spoken, so *Buon Appetito!*

Published in 2012 by Struik Lifestyle
(an imprint of Random House Struik (Pty) Ltd)
Company Reg. No. 1966/003153/07
Wembley Square, Solan Road, Gardens 8001
PO Box 1144, Cape Town, 8000, South Africa
www.randomstruik.co.za

PUBLISHER: Linda de Villiers
MANAGING EDITOR: Cecilia Barfield
EDITOR AND INDEXER: Bronwen Leak
DESIGNER: Beverley Dodd
PHOTOGRAPHER: Ryno
FOOD STYLIST: Brita du Plessis
FOOD STYLIST'S ASSISTANT: Yvette Pascoe
PROOFREADER: Gill Gordon
REPRODUCTION: Hirt & Carter Cape (Pty) Ltd
PRINTING AND BINDING: China

ISBN 978-1-77007-948-9 (Print)
ISBN 978-1-43230-017-3 (PDF)
ISBN 978-1-43230-055-5 (ePub)

Over 40 000 unique African images available to purchase from our image bank at www.imagesofafrica.co.za

Contents

Preface

The Vegetarian Kitchen is a vegetarian and lactose-free recipe book, which specifically highlights meals and recipes that do not rely on meat or dairy products to make them healthy or delicious. My intention is to showcase the simplicity of transforming a previously meat- and dairy-product laden diet into a purely vegetarian one. The concept of such a diet is quite foreign and indeed a little intimidating to many people who have consumed dairy products all their lives, and there really is no reason for this. Although cheese, for example, is a firm favourite with many people, once they realise that there are many alternative options, it becomes much easier to make that transition. Food is easy to prepare and once the concept of 'deprivation' has been abandoned, people realise just how many different types of meat- and dairy-free foods are actually available.

After having been quite an adept lacto-vegetarian cook for nearly ten years, it came as a shock to discover that my husband suffered from lactose intolerance, which loosely translates as the body's inability to digest dairy products. Thus we were forced to rethink the way we prepared our meals. Consequently we cut all dairy products out of our diet.

Lactose intolerance results in stomach disorders such as cramping, bloating and general discomfort, which can, in extreme cases, become quite severe.

It is thought that as many as 75 per cent of the world's population suffer from some form of lactose intolerance throughout their lives and is quite common in South Africa. There are many substitutes for dairy, and no aspect of cooking is out of reach of the dairy-free chef.

Life is about living in the moment and enjoying every day. In our stressful modern lifestyles, we don't always make time for the important things, and eating is one of them. Mealtimes should always reflect the values that our forefathers held dear – prepare food with love, and take time to eat and enjoy it. I want to bring across the feeling of lazy summer afternoons spent with loved ones over a delicious meal, which is no less tempting or enjoyable simply because there are no animal products in the dishes. I have discovered that many people are of the incorrect opinion that meat- and dairy-free means bland, tasteless and unappetising. Vegetarian food is not rabbit food, nor does it belong in the realms of the strange. It is not a 'new age' fad, but an ancient custom upheld by great men such as Pliny, Da Vinci and Einstein. It is simple, healthy and wholesome food, accessible to all who wish to make a change in their eating habits, whether for health, weight or ethical reasons.

The illustrations in this book are all my own, rendered in pen and ink, and are original drawings of the wonderful, delicious and colourful array of foods, herbs and spices that are available for us to eat.

I hope that this book shows you the joy of cooking, and how to return to basics and enjoy food that is meatless, dairy-free and delicious. And whether you are vegetarian or vegan for ethical reasons, lactose-intolerant, of a specific faith or religion that is intolerant of the consumption of animal products, or are simply following a healthier lifestyle and diet, there is something here for you. Even serious carnivores will find that food sans meat can be delicious and fulfilling, and just as comforting and hearty.

'CAPE TOWN FIRST CITY IN AFRICA TO ENDORSE A MEAT-FREE DAY A WEEK'

'On Tuesday, 6 April 2010 Compassion in World Farming managed to secure a first for Africa, with Cape Town's Health Portfolio Committee agreeing to officially endorse one meat-free day a week. This endorsement came shortly after the town of Ghent in Belguim made headline news in support of the cause. Government in Ghent have recognised the importance of promoting vegetarianism as a solution to addressing climate change and have declared one day a week "veggie" only day. And now many other cities have joined this campaign, including Sao Paulo in Brazil, Bremen in Germany, Baltimore and San Francisco in the USA, and cities in Croatia – and the list continues to grow.' (from Fry's Vegetarian: www.frysvegetarian.co.za)

MEAT-FREE MONDAYS

The Meat-free Mondays Campaign in South Africa has grown in leaps and bounds since its inception. Have a look at http://www.supportmfm.co.za and add your voice.

MELLISSA BUSHBY

Introduction

We live in a very beautiful part of the world, the Mpumalanga Lowveld, and our lives are spent in an idyll of not only what we feel like eating tonight, but what we feel like cooking. There is such pleasure in the eating, but also in the planning and especially in the making. There truly is nothing like baking bread from scratch – focaccia, slipper bread, herb bread, wholesome wholewheat seed bread, to mention just a few. And it really is so easy once you get the knack. I even bottle my own chillies and dry my own tomatoes (a healthy and delicious snack, especially if you have children). A friend told me a while ago that she wishes she had the time to do all that, especially bake bread. And I said, 'Why not?' We can all set aside the 10 or 15 minutes it takes to knead (very satisfying) a ball of dough. Then you leave it to stand, and it does most of the work on its own. It's easier than you think. And then there's the incomparable pleasure of enjoying the fruits of your labour. I always feel that as the baker, it is my privilege to eat the crust of freshly baked bread as it comes out of the oven. We were visiting friends a while back and I mentioned this to someone, and she promptly said, 'My husband doesn't bother waiting – he cuts off both of the crusts for himself, "because they are just wasted when not eaten straight from the oven!"'

So many of the foods we eat today are harmful to us, to our children and to the environment. My intention is to illustrate not only a healthier (and do not for one minute read bland or tasteless into that) way of eating, but also a way for the many vegetarian and lactose-intolerant people out there to see how easy it actually is to eat delicious, soul-satisfying food without meat or dairy. It involves, in large part, a mind-set adjustment; one has to not see it as a 'diet' (it's not) or as 'vegetarian' food – it is vegetarian, but only in that it does not contain animal products. For many centuries, many cultures ate a predominantly 'vegetarian' diet, quite simply because that was what they ate. If you had to ask them if they were vegetarian, they would have said no, certainly not. For me, after having been vegetarian for many years, adapting my diet to a dairy-free one was fairly easy. I have often been asked by meat-eating friends and family 'But what do you eat?' The simple truth is this – a lot more than we used to! You become far more adept at creating tasty, healthy (mostly), satisfying food, and cooking becomes such a pleasure. Who doesn't feel a certain satisfaction in creating a thick, hearty winter vegetable soup? Or at least relish the deep, glorious smell of one merrily bubbling away in the kitchen? Not to mention the pleasing aroma of the homemade crusty bread, made to mop up the soup, wafting through the house and warming it.

There are still people who believe we need meat to be healthy, but the truth is we don't. And for those who can't eat dairy products, due to health (or other) reasons, don't despair! We don't need dairy either. We have been vegetarian for many years, but we ate dairy products aplenty, and I noticed at times that after a particularly satisfying cheese-laden lasagne or cannelloni, my husband would complain of stomach cramps.

We eventually put two and two together, and did an experiment. He stopped eating cheese, all except for his absolute favourite, which was feta. All was well, for a while, and then it started happening again, so he gave up the feta (reluctantly, I can tell you). Quite a while passed, and then the cramps started up again. He decided to try giving up all dairy for a while, to see if it made any difference. I honestly could not believe that a few teaspoons of milk in tea or coffee could make any difference, but it did. He hasn't had any dairy for almost a year now, and his health has improved dramatically. And as hard as it was initially for him to give up cheese – this was a man who came home from work, took his tie off, went straight to the kitchen, cut half a slab of Cheddar and put it on a slice of bread – it is now a distant memory, and the thought of it no longer appeals to his tastes at all. And, because milk creates mucous, his sinuses have also cleared up. We adapted to not eating or drinking dairy products and now don't miss them, mostly because we have discovered that there are so many other delicious foods. I am not going to delve too deeply into all the health do's and don'ts of this, there are many excellent books on the subject, which I will mention at the end of this book. But this is a tale about food, and about eating and enjoying food. Pure and simple.

Think of the many countries in the world that eat a predominantly vegetarian diet, not because they are vegetarian, but for various other reasons: because meat is scarce and expensive, or veggies and other food types are plentiful and tasty, for ethical reasons or health, or even taste, as many people do not like the flavour, texture or idea of meat. In Italy, for example, there is such a huge variety of pasta, beans and pulses, grains and rice, not to mention the rich variety of seasonal fruits and vegetables, that meat becomes an 'optional extra' and, in fact, plays a very small role. And who can ever say that Italian food is not delicious! But it's not thought of as 'vegetarian' because, actually, it's not. The ingredients just don't include meat.

The same can be said of many other countries and their way of eating, such as China, the Middle East, Mexico and India. Many have their basic starch, which would be rice, pasta or corn, in the form of tortillas or breads, or various types of wheat breads and flatbreads. The meal could be a crisp vegetable stir-fry with marinated tofu, a rich tomato-based pasta with mushroom, chilli or garbanzo beans (chickpeas), a hearty potato or butternut curry, or satisfying black bean and corn chilli. There are endless salads, and dishes baked slowly in the time-honoured way, most easier and quicker to prepare than you would imagine. And there is something to be said for the Slow Food Movement, which teaches us to appreciate and deeply enjoy what we eat, to savour and really notice a hearty and satisfying dish, instead of rushing here and there. How many of us sit down with a glass of wine and enjoy every sip and every bite of the meal before us?

Many people, on seeing the word 'vegetarian', think the food bland or boring, and that they are being deprived by having to eat it, as a dieter feels deprived if their food is severely rationed. This is not so, and I want to prove it. Apart from ethical reasons – really, slaughterhouses are terrible places – there are millions of other reasons why we should follow a meatless diet. There are many people who no longer eat meat because of the awful suffering involved or because of the vast tracts of land being flattened so that cattle can be raised to feed the human hamburger fetish (don't get me wrong – I used to love hamburgers as much as the next, but there are many delicious alternatives to meat). Not to mention the health reasons, such as heart disease, dangerous cholesterol or blood-pressure, diabetes and obesity. My husband worked with a man who had been a big meat eater all his life, and he was diagnosed with severe cancer. He was put onto a strict vegan diet to save his life and, had he eaten differently during the course of his lifetime, he might have been a much healthier fellow.

More people are turning to an improved, aware, lifestyle. The medical fraternity is starting to increasingly acknowledge that the only thing meat does for you is to 'make you fat and harden your arteries'. And while it is still relatively difficult to eat a restaurant meal, for example, as a lactose-intolerant or vegan person, especially in South Africa, it is also becoming more and more commonplace. In fact, there is a growing trend towards people requesting that certain things that create allergies be omitted from a dish, such as fish, eggs or nuts. There are thousands of people who cannot, or do not, for whatever reason, eat any animal products.

This book is an expedition into a world of delicious food and pleasurable cooking, with ideas taken from all over the world and made in our very own, South African way. I hope it's a journey of awareness and discovery, one that will show you just how easy it is to 'satisfy a big hunger' without meat and dairy, and to enjoy every tasty morsel. And because veggies, pulses, legumes and the like have no heart-clogging fat, you can enjoy an extra sorbet, or maybe two.

Please note that dairy products can replace the soya products (for example milk) in any of these recipes. Quantities remain the same.

Enjoy the journey, and indulge!

The Essential Store Cupboard

In this book, I have mentioned the brand names that I use at home, although, if there are specific brands that you prefer, I don't believe it will make any difference to the end product, so feel free to experiment. Also, I have deliberated long and hard about whether or not to include 'meat substitutes' (such as soya mince). These items do have their place on our table, for a quick spaghetti bolognaise, Tex-Mex pizza or mince pie, for instance, but lentils will do just as well. So it is up to you whether you put in soya mince or lentils. They are fairly interchangeable in that both go well in cottage pie, bolognaise or lasagne. There are soya mince varieties available that are healthy as well as tasty, one of them being Nature's Choice. Don't even attempt the 'cardboard' tasting varieties! Look in your local health shop or the larger Spar stores. A further option worth trying is Fry's Vegetarian, a local brand specialising in meat-free 'meat' products, such as hot dogs, burger patties, sausages, prepared mince and chunky strips.

Another substitute I deliberated over is soya milk as a milk alternative. Personally, I am not a fan of the majority of soya milks, but if, like me, you cannot survive without numerous cups of tea, I do find the powdered soya milk far superior to the carton, although it is best to make it up in a blender, and not just add the powder as you would a coffee creamer. Always remember to stir well or give the carton a good shake before use. Having said that, there are ready-made soya milk brands available that are just as good, although you may spend a little more. Examples are Woolworths Organic Soya Milk, Alpro and Good Hope. Soya cream is also available, and is just as good as, if not better than, the original. There are also soya yoghurts and various brands of dairy-free ice cream on the market. And a wonderful thing for Irish Coffee is Orley Whip, which is also excellent for baking. Check the label; a lot of soya milks are fortified with calcium, Vitamin B12 (very important) and protein, so you don't miss out on any of the health benefits, without the fat. Of course, there are other options available too, such as rice and almond milk.

The following are essential store-cupboard ingredients that you should never be without.

DRIED PASTA

Spaghetti, macaroni, penne or rigatoni, bavette or linguine, shells, lasagne sheets – we always have a wide variety on hand. Pasta always comes in handy in a pinch, to throw into a soup or to whip up a quick last-minute Sunday night meal.

PULSES AND LEGUMES

This is an important one. ALWAYS have lentils (black, green, brown and red), green split peas, beans (my favourite are red kidney beans), super-proteined soya beans and meaty-tasting borlotti, or sugar, beans on hand. The small white beans, called haricot, are very good in tomato sauce, and are a good old South African favourite. If you can find them, adzuki beans are also a good standby. Although a bit more expensive, they are packed full of nutrients, as are black beans.

Most important of all (I think so, anyway), are the sweet, small, wrinkled orbs called ceci, garbanzos or, more commonly, chickpeas. These are wonderful for many things, the least of which is hummus. They are also excellent in an apple curry. Barley is another must, and so is rice – brown and/or wild, and basmati. I make my own soup mix (see page 164), but store-bought is fine.

Pulses, legumes and grains are an important source of protein and carbohydrates for vegetarians, and they are versatile, economical and nutritious.

I always do extra beans, in fact I make up the whole packet and simply freeze the extra. That way I always have beans ready for use; they just have to be defrosted, which some hot water does quite effectively. I do the same thing with chickpeas; boil them up and freeze them, so that their delightful tastes are always available. But don't throw away the water used to boil them – it is a thick, gelatinous stock-like liquid that can be used in soups, curries, stews and the like.

NUTS AND SEEDS

A rich source of fat and protein, nuts are good to have on standby; my favourites are cashews, almonds, pistachios and pecans. The seeds I use most are sunflower, linseeds and sesame (refrigerate them to preserve their Vitamin E content).

CANNED GOODS

Keep good-quality canned tomatoes, both whole and chopped, as well as a can or two of tomato purée. Tomato paste is also a must, either canned or in a tube. And, while we are on the topic, good-old All Gold tomato sauce is an essential, I use it all the time. Also have a few cans of chickpeas on standby, as well as a can or two of butter beans and kidney beans. And some jam, for the occasional jam tart. Coconut milk and coconut cream are also nice to have when there is a Thai curry (or homemade ice cream) on the menu.

VINEGARS AND OILS

Apple cider, red wine and grape vinegar are all used for different purposes, and should always be on hand. Also important to have is balsamic vinegar, a must for a light drizzling over salads and soups. Not essential, but nice to have, are infused oils and vinegars. These are very easy to make yourself, such as garlic- and rosemary-infused olive oil and vinegar. Olive oil, extra-virgin if possible, is used quite lavishly in our house, although hardly ever to cook with. For the very health conscious, a little stock can, in most cases, be used to shallow-fry certain foods.

I often interchange sunflower and canola oil, either one can be used in nearly every case. When I mention olive oil, it is always extra-virgin, the best that you can afford. And remember that it is better not to cook with what the Italians affectionately call 'green gold', although I do sometimes use it for the sheer taste of it, when nothing else will do.

HERBS AND SPICES

Origanum, basil and parsley are my standby herbs, although I do use rosemary on breads. Please note that while these herbs are dried, fresh is just as good, probably better. A rule of thumb when substituting is to double the amount of dried if using fresh or halve the amount of fresh if substituting dried.

Paprika, cayenne pepper, ground ginger, cumin, coriander (ground and seeds), turmeric, mustard seeds and ground cinnamon are all important to have in the spice rack. Bay leaves, a good curry powder and a homemade masala are also useful. Vegetable stock is a necessity too, cubes or powder, as well as salt and pepper. I use both coarse and fine sea salt, and mostly cracked black pepper (a fancy way of saying ground, although it can also be 'cracked' in a mortar and pestle).

Garlic is a must. I am going to mention it here, even though technically it falls under 'fresh' ingredients and not store cupboard. I always have a jar of ready-crushed garlic in the fridge and a good helping of heads sitting on my kitchen counter. They are quite easy to peel if you know the trick – put the individual clove on a chopping board and press down hard on it with the flat side of a chopping knife to crush it lightly. You can then peel; the skin comes off very easily.

MISCELLANEOUS

I keep plain white or bread flour, wholewheat flour for breads and pizzas, and cake flour for cakes and tarts. Also needed are dried yeast, castor sugar, icing sugar, vanilla essence, cocoa powder, baking powder and bicarbonate of soda, a wonder ingredient used for all sorts of things around the house.

Other ingredients can be used for a bit of variety. You can, for example, substitute two stock cubes with 5 ml (1 tsp) Marmite; this is especially nice in soups. Molasses or treacle can be used instead of sugar in cakes, stews and even sauces.

Another important store-cupboard ingredient is bottled lemon juice, for when fresh lemons are not available or just too much effort to squeeze.

VEGETABLES

The absolute essentials are onions, garlic and tomatoes. Almost as important are potatoes, celery, butternut and/or pumpkin, carrots, chillies, peppers and aubergines. Also, always have fresh lemons if possible.

So, that's that. All you need to get started on a delectable taste adventure. You do not need fancy, specialised ingredients to eat wholesome vegetarian and dairy-free food. There are occasional things that are not everyday items, such as nutritional yeast, but none are essential and can easily be done without or exchanged for something else.

Light Meals & Sides

For those long and lazy summer days, when all you can do is graze idly while the world glides by.

We often sit outside on our stoep in the early evening, our table laden with crunchy salads and delicious

toasted bruschetta with marinated mushrooms, or tomato and basil drizzled with peppery olive oil.

Rich and creamy hummus, with crispy vegetable chips dipped in sweet and sour chilli sauce,

all washed down with something cold and icy like homemade lemonade or a good old-fashioned G & T.

Everything in this chapter can be eaten as an accompaniment or as a snack, be it for a picnic, a side dish

to a main meal, a nibble on the beach or a bite around the braai. It depends on the day, the occasion,

the mood and, of course, the level of hunger. Also, many of them are neatly disguised as 'grown-up' food,

but really, children love them too, especially the aubergine slices, pastry tarts and the different types of fritters.

Deep-fried Vegetables in Batter

250 ml (1 cup) chana flour (chickpea flour)
375 ml (1½ cup) water
5 ml (1 tsp) turmeric
juice of 1 lemon or lime, or 15 ml (1 Tbsp) fresh lemon or lime juice
5 ml (1 tsp) chilli powder or flakes (or to taste)
assorted vegetables (broccoli and cauliflower florets, aubergine slices, carrot sticks, mushrooms, green beans, etc.)
oil for deep-frying

1. Mix the flour, water, turmeric, lemon or lime juice and chilli powder. The consistency should be that of thick cream.
2. Dip the vegetables into the batter and deep-fry in hot oil until crispy. Drain on absorbent paper towel.
3. Serve warm with a dipping sauce like sweet and sour sauce (see page 148) or a mayonnaise dip.

SERVES 4

Vegetable Tartlets

1 x 400 g roll shortcrust pastry
30 ml (2 Tbsp) vegetable oil
1 onion, peeled and diced
10 ml (2 tsp) crushed garlic
2 chillies, chopped
1 red and 1 yellow pepper, seeded and diced
a good handful of green beans, chopped (about ¾ cup)
2 carrots, peeled and grated
2 tomatoes, chopped
salt and pepper to taste
30 ml (2 Tbsp) olive oil

1. Preheat the oven to 180 °C.
2. Grease and flour two tartlet or muffin tins.
3. Roll out the pastry and cut 24 rounds. Press the rounds into the tins to line the base and sides. Prick each round lightly with a fork a few times, and bake blind for about 5 minutes. Note that baking blind normally involves putting dried beans or rice inside the pastry case to prevent it puffing, but in this case the holes made by the fork should allow the air to escape.
4. Meanwhile, heat the vegetable oil in a frying pan and sauté the onion, garlic and chilli. Add the peppers and beans, and stir. Simmer for 5 minutes.
5. Add the carrots and tomatoes, and cook for a further 5–10 minutes. Season well with salt and pepper.
6. Spoon the mixture into the pastry cases and bake for 5 minutes.
7. Remove from the oven and drizzle with the olive oil before serving.

MAKES 24

Deep-fried Vegetables in Batter

Onion Tarts

Onion Tarts

3–4 onions, peeled and sliced
15 ml (1 Tbsp) sunflower oil
1 x 400 g roll puff pastry
salt and pepper to taste
a drizzle of balsamic vinegar
a drizzle of olive oil
thyme for garnishing

1. Preheat the oven to 220 °C.
2. Fry the onions in the sunflower oil until soft and translucent.
3. While the onions are cooking, roll out the pastry to a thickness of 5 mm, divide into four equal rectangles and arrange on a baking tray.
4. Spread the onions over the pastry and season with salt and pepper.
5. Drizzle balsamic vinegar and olive oil over the top and bake for 10–15 minutes, until risen and golden brown. Garnish and serve.

MAKES 4

Butternut Fritters

The following fritter recipes are excellent for children, who love the making just as much as the eating, so let them help. They are delicious whether eaten hot or cold, and will complement any meal. Just as easily, they stand alone as a snack on the picnic table.

1 small butternut, peeled and cubed
2–3 cloves garlic, peeled
60 ml (¼ cup) vegetable oil
2 medium–large potatoes, peeled
2 courgettes, grated
1 stale bread roll, crumbled
1 onion, peeled and finely diced
2.5 ml (½ tsp) ground cumin
salt and pepper to taste

1. Preheat the oven to 200 °C.
2. Arrange the butternut and garlic in a roasting pan and drizzle over half of the vegetable oil. Roast for approximately 45 minutes, until tender and sweet.
3. Meanwhile, parboil the potatoes.
4. Blend the roasted butternut and garlic, potatoes, courgettes and bread in a blender until combined. Stir in the onion, cumin, salt and pepper.
5. Heat the remaining vegetable oil in a non-stick frying pan and drop in spoonfuls of the butternut mixture. Allow the fritters time to cook through on the bottom before being tempted to turn them over, otherwise they will fall apart; this takes 3–5 minutes. The sides will start to crisp and there will be no resistance when you slide a spatula underneath to flip them over. Turn and fry on the other side until crispy. Drain on paper towels.

MAKES 8 LARGE OR 10 SMALL

Sweet Potato and Courgette Fritters

2 large sweet potatoes, peeled
4–5 courgettes
1 stale bread slice or roll
15 ml (1 Tbsp) cornflour
5 ml (1 tsp) salt
5 ml (1 tsp) sugar
2.5 ml (½ tsp) each of ground ginger, paprika and turmeric
15 ml (1 Tbsp) chopped fresh parsley or 5 ml (1 tsp) dried
1 onion, peeled and finely diced
30–45 ml (2–3 Tbsp) olive oil

1. Grate the potatoes and courgettes into a colander and steam for 15 minutes over a pot of boiling water.
2. Preheat the oven to 200 °C.
3. Put the steamed potatoes and courgettes in a blender with the bread and cornflour, and blend until combined. The mixture can be quite smooth or still a bit chunky if preferred.
4. Transfer to a bowl and stir in the salt, sugar, spices, parsley and onion.
5. Grease or line a baking tray with baking paper and place tablespoonfuls of the mixture onto the tray.
6. Lightly squash them with a fork, and drizzle with olive oil. Bake for 25 minutes until firm, resisting the urge to turn them over before this.
7. When they are quite firm, flip them over and bake for a further 15 minutes, or until crispy. Serve with a dipping sauce of your choice.

MAKES 8

Sweetcorn, Rice and Courgette Patties

As with the butternut and sweet potato fritters (see page 15 and above), children love this recipe, so let them help with the preparation. Be warned though, it can become quite messy!

4 small or 3 medium courgettes, grated
375 ml (1½ cups) cooked brown rice
1 x 410 g can creamstyle sweetcorn
5 ml (1 tsp) ground ginger
5 ml (1 tsp) paprika
5 ml (1 tsp) salt
250 ml (1 cup) breadcrumbs
30 ml (2 Tbsp) chickpea flour
30 ml (2 Tbsp) olive or avocado oil (optional)
1 onion, peeled and diced
30 ml (2 Tbsp) chopped fresh parsley or 10 ml (2 tsp) dried
cake flour for dusting
sunflower oil for baking

1. Combine all the ingredients, except the onion and parsley, in a bowl.
2. Divide the mixture in half and blend one half in a blender. Stir this into the remaining half of the mixture and mix in the onion and parsley.
3. Shape into patties (I usually make them about the size of my palm), using flour both on your hands and a little on a plate to prevent them from sticking. If the mixture is too 'sloppy', add more breadcrumbs or flour. If the mixture is a bit dry, add more olive or avocado oil.
4. Place the patties on a floured baking tray. Allow to stand, preferably in the fridge, for about 20 minutes.
5. Preheat the oven to 180 °C.
6. Drizzle the patties with a little sunflower oil and bake for about 20 minutes, until slightly crispy.

MAKES 6–8

Tomato and Onion Squares

Tomato and Onion Squares

2–3 cloves garlic, crushed
3 tomatoes, roughly chopped
5 ml (1 tsp) dried or chopped fresh rosemary
5 ml (1 tsp) dried sweet basil
30 ml (2 Tbsp) capers
1 x 400 g roll puff pastry
2 onions, peeled and sliced
30 ml (2 Tbsp) olive oil
30 ml (2 Tbsp) balsamic vinegar
coarse sea salt and cracked black pepper to taste

1. Preheat the oven to 200 °C.
2. Mix the garlic, tomatoes, herbs and capers in a bowl. Allow to rest while preparing the pastry.
3. Roll out the pastry and cut into 12 squares of 6 cm each.
4. Arrange the sliced onion and the tomato mixture on the squares, drizzle with the olive oil and balsamic vinegar, and season with salt and pepper.
5. Bake for roughly 20 minutes until the pastry is golden brown.

MAKES 12

Monsoon Pancakes

Traditionally from India, these 'crêpes' are delicious made with a filling of either lightly fried onions, mushrooms and spinach, creamed mushrooms or creamed spinach. You could also make a tomato and onion gravy, or the good-old South African favourite, 'Shiva' sauce.

250 g rice flour
5 ml (1 tsp) baking powder
10 ml (2 tsp) sugar
2.5 ml (½ tsp) paprika
2.5 ml (½ tsp) turmeric
250 ml (1 cup) coconut milk
2.5 ml (½ tsp) salt
250 ml (1 cup) water
5 ml (1 tsp) vegetable oil

1. Blend all the ingredients, except the oil, into a batter with the consistency of thick cream, adding a little extra water if necessary.
2. Heat the oil in a non-stick frying pan and pour approximately 80 ml (⅓ cup) of the batter into the pan at a time, swirling to create a uniform, fairly thin pancake.
3. Fry until golden brown on both sides and the edges are crispy.
4. Use your choice of filling. To make the creamed spinach and mushroom fillings, lightly fry sliced mushrooms or chopped spinach, turn down the heat and slowly pour in the desired amount of non-dairy cream, depending on the quantity of spinach or mushrooms used.

MAKES 6–8

Mustard-glazed Veggies

200 g carrots, peeled and julienned
200 g green beans, diced
chopped fresh coriander to garnish
salt and pepper to taste

DRESSING:
45 ml (3 Tbsp) olive oil
15 ml (1 Tbsp) apple cider vinegar
2.5 ml (½ tsp) sugar
10 ml (2 tsp) Dijon mustard

1. Lightly steam the carrots and beans.
2. Whisk or blend the dressing ingredients together.
3. Pour the dressing over the vegetables, garnish with coriander, and season with salt and pepper. Serve warm.

SERVES 4

Frijoles Refritos (Refried Beans)

There are quite a few different takes on this recipe. This is a basic foundation, but with some chopped carrots and green beans added in, it can become more of a main than a snack. A fresh, crisp garden salad will round it off as a complete meal. Alternatively, add a little more stock and spoon the beans over hearty brown rice.

30–45 ml (2–3 Tbsp) sunflower or canola oil
1 onion, peeled and diced
crushed garlic to taste
2–3 chillies, chopped
250 ml (1 cup) prepared kidney beans or
1 x 410 g can kidney beans
30–45 ml (2–3 Tbsp) water or
vegetable stock (optional)
salt and pepper to taste

1. Heat the oil in a frying pan and fry the onion, garlic and chillies.
2. Add the beans and mash them using the back of a fork or a potato masher. Consistency is to your preference, but they should still retain some chunkiness.
3. Add a little water or vegetable stock if the mixture is too thick.
4. Season with salt and pepper, and serve with crusty bread or pita wedges drizzled with olive oil, and a salsa.

SERVES 2 AS A MAIN OR 4 AS A SIDE OR SNACK

Mustard-glazed Veggies

Pesto Mushrooms

Pesto Mushrooms

16 medium or 8 large mushrooms (any kind), stalks removed
60 ml (¼ cup) olive oil
30 ml (2 Tbsp) pesto (see page 153)
5 ml (1 tsp) crushed garlic
30 ml (2 Tbsp) chopped fresh parsley

1. Preheat the oven to 200 °C. Lightly oil an ovenproof dish large enough to hold the mushrooms in a single layer.
2. Place the mushrooms in the dish and drizzle over the olive oil.
3. Mix the pesto and garlic together and spoon over the mushrooms.
4. Bake for 30 minutes. Pour off the excess mushroom water and scatter over the parsley before serving.

SERVES 4

Mint Beans

350–400 g green beans, washed
45–60 ml (3–4 Tbsp) olive oil
juice of ½ lemon
a handful of chopped fresh mint leaves

1. Blanch the beans in salted boiling water until *al dente*.
2. Drain and toss with the olive oil, lemon juice and mint.

SERVES 4

Crispy Fried Green Beans

125 ml (½ cup) vegetable oil
350 g green beans, washed and dried
coarse sea salt and cracked black pepper to taste

1. Heat the oil in a wok.
2. When lightly smoking, toss the green beans in the oil and stir continuously for even frying.
3. Once the beans are crispy, remove from the oil and drain. Season well with salt and pepper.

SERVES 4

Lemon and Garlic Spinach

1 x 250 g pkt baby spinach
60 ml (¼ cup) olive oil
5 ml (1 tsp) crushed garlic
juice of ½ lemon
coarse sea salt and cracked black pepper
to taste
30–45 ml (2–3 Tbsp) chopped
pecans (optional)

1. Steam the spinach until just wilted.
2. Heat 15–30 ml (1–2 Tbsp) of the oil and sauté the garlic.
3. Gently fold in the spinach to combine.
4. Squeeze over the lemon juice, add the remaining oil, and season with salt and pepper.
5. Stir to combine and sprinkle over the chopped nuts, if using.

SERVES 2–4

Battered Aubergine Slices

These are delicious the next day as a snack, and children love them.

15 ml (1 Tbsp) lemon juice
250 ml (1 cup) soya milk
5 ml (1 tsp) each of dried basil, parsley
and origanum
5ml (1 tsp) each of paprika, ground ginger
and cumin
2.5 ml (½ tsp) each of cayenne pepper,
turmeric, salt and pepper
250 ml (1 cup) cake flour
125 ml (½ cup) semolina
2 large aubergines, sliced
60–125 ml (¼–½ cup) sunflower oil

1. Stir the lemon juice into the milk and allow to stand for 10 minutes.
2. In a bowl, mix the herbs, spices, flour and semolina.
3. Dip the aubergine slices into the flour mixture, then into the milk, then again into the flour.
4. Heat the oil in a frying pan and shallow-fry the slices in batches, on both sides, until crispy on the outside and soft inside.
5. Serve warm.

MAKES 14–16

Roast Pumpkin Wedges

Crumbed Mushrooms

250 ml (1 cup) cake flour
10 ml (2 tsp) paprika
2.5 ml (½ tsp) cracked black pepper
5 ml (1 tsp) dried mixed herbs
5 ml (1 tsp) salt
250 ml (1 cup) soya milk
500 g button mushrooms
oil for deep-frying

1. Combine the flour, paprika, pepper, mixed herbs and salt in a shallow bowl.
2. Pour the milk into another bowl and dunk each mushroom in it.
3. Roll the mushrooms in the flour mixture until evenly coated and allow to stand, in the fridge, for 30 minutes.
4. Deep-fry the mushrooms in oil until golden brown.
5. Place onto paper towels to absorb the excess oil and serve immediately, topped with garlic 'butter' (see page 157) or with herb mayonnaise for dipping.

SERVES 4

Roast Pumpkin Wedges

½ pumpkin, unpeeled and cut into wedges
3 red peppers, seeded and halved
3 red onions, peeled and quartered
60 ml (¼ cup) maple syrup
30 ml (2 Tbsp) balsamic vinegar
30 ml (2 Tbsp) olive oil
salt and pepper to taste

1. Preheat the oven to 180 °C. Place the pumpkin, peppers and onions in a large baking dish.
2. Drizzle the syrup, vinegar and olive oil over the top and stir to ensure all the vegetables are evenly coated.
3. Roast for 30–40 minutes until browned and caramelised.
4. Season with salt and pepper, and serve warm.

SERVES 4–6

Roast Potato Bites

6 medium potatoes, unpeeled and cubed
3–4 sprigs fresh rosemary or
10 ml (2 tsp) dried
6 whole cloves garlic
15 ml (1 Tbsp) coarse sea salt
60 ml (¼ cup) olive oil

1. Preheat the oven to 200 °C.
2. Toss all the ingredients together in a bowl, mixing well to ensure the potato is evenly coated in the oil.
3. Roast on a baking tray for about 40 minutes, until golden and sizzling.

SERVES 4

Spiced Potato Wedges

Whether you prefer thick, chunky wedges or slim, delicate fingers (which would require less time in the oven), these are always a winner with young and old alike. After all, who doesn't love potato chips? Especially when they are just as delicious baked as they are fried. The cayenne pepper can be omitted completely, especially for children who don't like spicy chips.

7–8 medium potatoes
60 ml (¼ cup) vegetable oil
coarse sea salt and cracked black pepper
to taste
10 ml (2 tsp) paprika
2.5 ml (½ tsp) cayenne pepper (optional)

1. Preheat the oven to 200 °C. Line a baking tray with baking paper.
2. Wash the potatoes, cut in half lengthways, and then in half again.
3. Put the wedges into a large bowl and pour over the oil. Season with salt and pepper, and add the paprika and cayenne pepper, if using. Mix well with a wooden spoon or spatula to make sure the spices are evenly distributed.
4. Place the wedges in a single layer on the baking tray and bake for 1½–2 hours, stirring every now and then.

SERVES 4–6

Roast Onions

Roast Onions

4 onions, unpeeled and halved
250 ml (1 cup) red wine vinegar
60 ml (¼ cup) olive oil
45–60 ml (3–4 Tbsp) crushed garlic

1. Preheat the oven to 220 °C.
2. Marinade the onions in the vinegar for 30 minutes, then place in a roasting pan. Spoon the vinegar over the onions to baste.
3. Drizzle with the oil and spoon over the garlic.
4. Roast for 1 hour or until the onions are soft and caramelised.

SERVES 4–6

Curried Yellow Rice

45 ml (3 Tbsp) olive oil
1 onion, peeled and chopped
10 ml (2 tsp) crushed garlic
10 ml (2 tsp) curry powder
10 ml (2 tsp) turmeric
375 ml (1½ cups) brown rice
750 ml (3 cups) water
10 ml (2 tsp) salt

1. Heat the oil in a heavy-bottomed saucepan and fry the onion and garlic until softened.
2. Add the curry powder, turmeric and rice, and cook, stirring, for 2 minutes. Add the water and salt, and bring to the boil, uncovered.
3. Reduce the heat, cover with a lid and simmer for 30–40 minutes, until the rice is cooked and steam holes appear on the surface of the grains.
4. Remove from the heat and allow to stand for 5 minutes, covered, before fluffing up with a fork.

SERVES 4

Onion Rings

1 kg large white onions, peeled
250 ml (1 cup) cake flour
5 ml (1 tsp) salt
2.5 ml (½ tsp) fine-ground black pepper
10 ml (2 tsp) either paprika or cayenne pepper
(depending on hot or not)
oil for deep-frying

1. Slice the onions into 1 cm-thick wheels.
2. Place in a medium-sized freezer bag (large enough to hold all the ingredients with room to move).
3. In a bowl, thoroughly mix the flour, salt, pepper and spice, and add this to the bag of onions.
4. Tightly seal the bag and shake until the onions are completely coated.
5. Remove the onions from the bag and place directly into hot oil.
6. Deep-fry until golden brown and drain on paper towel.
7. Serve warm (but they are also excellent cold).

SERVES 4–6

The Best Ever Roast Potatoes

12 medium potatoes, peeled and halved
30 ml (2 Tbsp) cornflour
200 ml sunflower or canola oil
5 ml (1 tsp) vegetable salt
5 ml (1 tsp) dried mixed herbs
5 ml (1 tsp) paprika
coarse sea salt and cracked black pepper
to taste

1. Preheat the oven to 200 °C. Lightly oil a baking dish.
2. Place the potatoes in a pot with enough water to cover them. Bring to the boil, then reduce the heat and simmer for 15–20 minutes, until they just start to soften around the edges. Drain and leave in the pot.
3. Sprinkle the cornflour over the potatoes, place the lid on the pot and shake well to coat.
4. Spread the potatoes evenly in the baking dish and drizzle with the oil. Sprinkle over the vegetable salt, herbs and paprika, and season with salt and pepper.
5. Roast for 45–60 minutes or until browned, crisp and sizzling.

SERVES 4–6

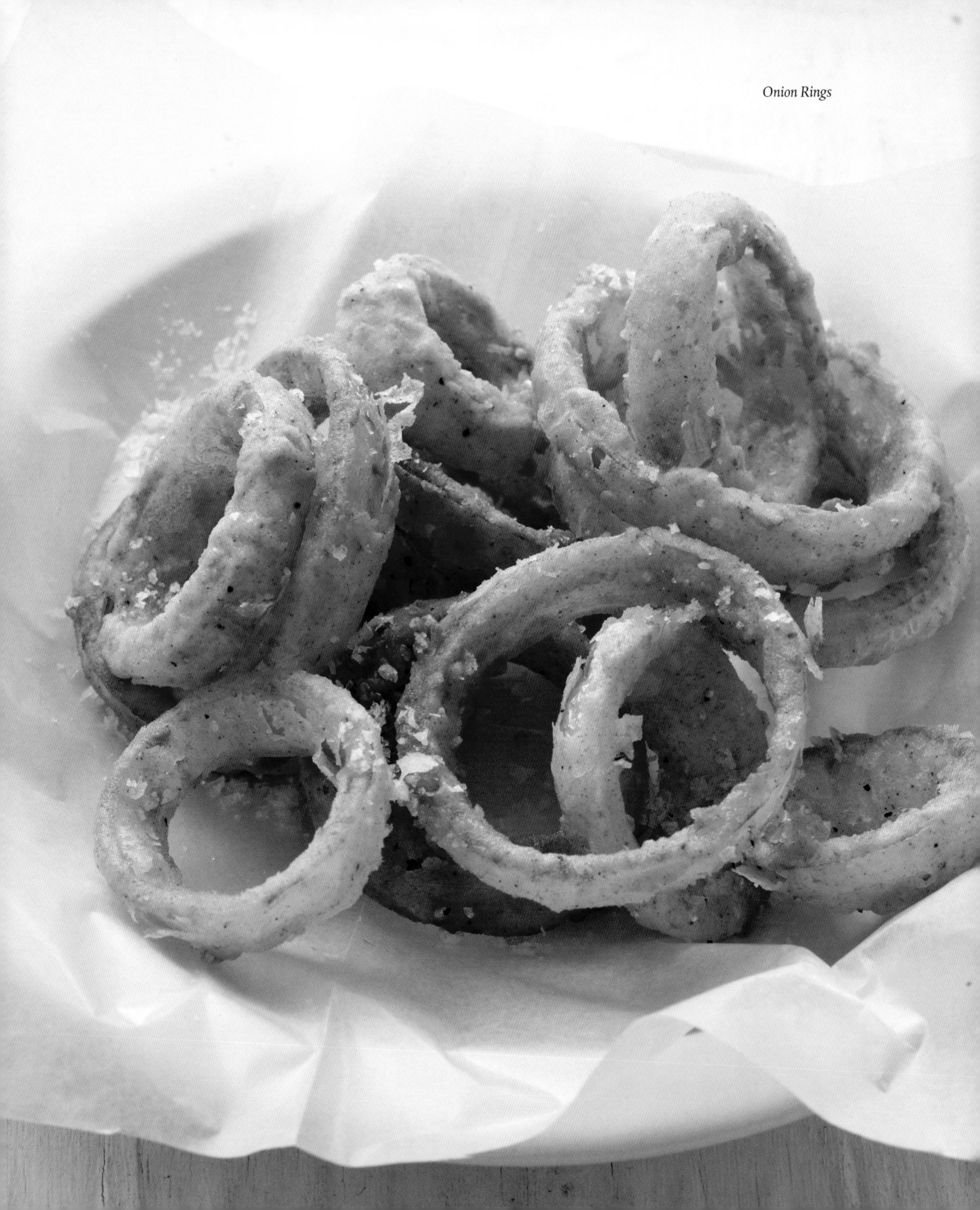

Onion Rings

Salads & Soups

I love salads; their crisp freshness, their light and zesty way of filling a gap that isn't quite filled by a meal,

and the way they round off everything. And in summer, when it gets so hot that even the ever-busy bees are sleepy

and lethargic, and no one wants to eat a warm, heavy meal, a cool and refreshing salad always fits the bill

(and fills the gap). Despite their light freshness, some salads really are a 'main meal', especially pasta or rice salads,

and they are invariably healthy as well as tasty. So, there is always room for a salad.

On the other hand, a deeply satisfying, heart-warming soup is, in my opinion, the only good thing about winter.

Hearty and chunky or silky and smooth, soup is the backbone of many a happy home. Our household

would not survive without soup, eaten with homemade, crusty bread; we eat soup as if it were going out of fashion,

especially on cold and rainy days, throughout the dreary winter months. But why keep soup for winter only?

A warming butternut and ginger, spicy tomato or rich and earthy lentil soup,

is good all year round, no matter the weather.

Roast Beetroot and Spinach Salad

8 small beetroot, trimmed and washed
60 ml (¼ cup) olive oil
50 g baby spinach leaves
15 ml (1 Tbsp) finely diced fresh chillies
6 spring onions, chopped
sea salt and cracked black pepper to taste
20 ml (4 tsp) balsamic vinegar
60 ml (¼ cup) roughly chopped fresh parsley

1. Preheat the oven to 180 °C.
2. Cook the beetroot in salted water for approximately 25 minutes, until just tender. Drain and cool. Peel and halve the beetroot. Place in a roasting pan, drizzle with half the olive oil, and roast for 20–30 minutes.
3. Mix together the roast beetroot, spinach, chillies and spring onions, and place on a platter. Season with salt and pepper, drizzle with the balsamic vinegar and remaining olive oil, and scatter the parsley over the top.

SERVES 4

Salatet Batata (Potato Salad)

Inspired by the Middle East, we now don't enjoy the 'traditional' potato salad as much as this one without mayonnaise.

3–4 potatoes, peeled and cubed
15 ml (1 Tbsp) chopped fresh parsley
6 spring onions, chopped

DRESSING:
5 ml (1 tsp) crushed garlic
5 ml (1 tsp) salt
45 ml (3 Tbsp) olive oil
30 ml (2 Tbsp) lemon juice
15 ml (1 Tbsp) cider vinegar
sea salt and cracked black pepper to taste

1. Boil the potatoes in salted water until cooked and allow to cool.
2. Mix the dressing ingredients in a bowl and allow to stand for 20–30 minutes.
3. Place the cooled potatoes in a serving bowl, pour over the dressing and shake or gently stir to coat. If you want a little more dressing over the potatoes, add some more lemon juice and olive oil.
4. Season with a little extra salt and pepper, and top with the chopped parsley and spring onions.

SERVES 4

Roast Beetroot and Spinach Salad

Bean Salad

Bean Salad

This is excellent eaten with fresh, crusty homemade bread or used as a bruschetta topping.

250 ml (1 cup) prepared kidney beans or
1 x 410 g can kidney beans, drained
1 onion, peeled and diced
2 carrots, peeled and sliced
¼ cucumber, chopped
125 ml (½ cup) chopped fresh parsley
30 ml (2 Tbsp) lemon juice
30 ml (2 Tbsp) cider vinegar
45–60 ml (3–4 Tbsp) olive oil
salt and black pepper to taste

1. Mix all the ingredients in a bowl and allow to stand in the fridge for about 1 hour before serving.

SERVES 4

Coleslaw

¼ cabbage, grated
½ large onion, peeled and finely chopped
2 carrots, peeled and grated
30 ml (2 Tbsp) lemon juice
30 ml (2 Tbsp) grape vinegar
30 ml (2 Tbsp) apple cider vinegar
5 ml (1 tsp) sugar
salt and black pepper to taste
a good glug of olive oil over the top

1. Thoroughly mix all the ingredients together and allow to stand for 15 minutes.

SERVES 4

Note: For a more traditional coleslaw, omit the apple cider vinegar and 15 ml (1 Tbsp) of the grape vinegar, and instead add 60 ml (¼ cup) mayonnaise.

Noodle Salad

2 x 200 g pkts ready-to-cook Hokkien or Pad
Thai noodles
6–8 spring onions, chopped

DRESSING:
45 ml (3 Tbsp) peanut butter
10 ml (2 tsp) chopped fresh garlic
10 ml (2 tsp) finely grated fresh ginger
5 ml (1 tsp) chilli sauce
15 ml (1 Tbsp) cider vinegar
15 ml (1 Tbsp) soy sauce
30 ml (2 Tbsp) sesame or sunflower oil
10 ml (2 tsp) sugar
salt and black pepper to taste

1. Cook the noodles according to the packet instructions. Place the cooked noodles in a serving bowl.
2. Stir all the dressing ingredients together and pour over the noodles.
3. Allow to cool and sprinkle over the chopped spring onions. Serve cold.

SERVES 4–6

Kidney Bean Salad

1 x 410 g can kidney beans or 250 ml (1 cup)
precooked kidney beans
1 x 410 g can whole kernel corn
1 red pepper, seeded and sliced
juice of 1 orange
30 ml (2 Tbsp) balsamic vinegar
30 ml (2 Tbsp) olive oil
salt and black pepper to taste
1 avocado, thinly sliced
15 ml (1 Tbsp) fresh lemon juice

1. Combine the beans, corn and red pepper in a salad bowl.
2. Pour the orange juice, balsamic vinegar and olive oil over the salad and season to taste.
3. Allow to stand in the fridge for about 1 hour for the flavours to develop.
4. Just before serving, top with the thinly sliced avocado and lemon juice.

SERVES 4

Apple and Chilli Salad

Apple and Chilli Salad

3 apples, unpeeled and chopped (you can also
use spanspek or melon)
15 ml (1 Tbsp) capers or finely
chopped gherkin
2–3 red chillies, diced
juice and zest of 2 limes
3–4 spring onions, chopped
a handful of fresh rocket
salt and black pepper to taste
45 ml (3 Tbsp) olive oil

1. Toss all the ingredients together.
2. Chill slightly and serve just below room temperature.

SERVES 4

Wild Rice Medley

250 ml (1 cup) brown and wild rice
1–2 mealies, kernels removed
5 ml (1 tsp) paprika
30 ml (2 Tbsp) sunflower oil
5 ml (1 tsp) coarse sea salt
125 ml (½ cup) lightly crushed pecans
1 red onion, peeled and thinly sliced
1 ripe avocado, diced
30–45 ml (2–3 Tbsp) red wine vinegar
30–45 ml (2–3 Tbsp) extra-virgin olive oil
125 ml (½ cup) chopped fresh coriander
1 chilli, finely sliced (optional)
salt and black pepper to taste

1. Cook the rice according to the packet instructions.
2. Lightly toss the corn kernels with the paprika, oil and salt, and gently toast in a hot oven. They must be crispy and a little charred in parts, but not burnt.
3. Allow the rice and corn to cool slightly.
4. When cool, stir the corn, nuts and onion into the rice. Fold the avocado into the salad (gently – do not be overzealous or you may end up with avocado mash).
5. Transfer to a serving bowl and drizzle over the red wine vinegar and olive oil. Top with the coriander and chilli (if using), and season to taste.

SERVES 4

Pasta Salad

1 x 500 g pkt fusilli or pasta shells
6 spring onions, diced
2 carrots, peeled and julienned
1 red onion, peeled and sliced
¼ cucumber, finely sliced
juice of ½ lemon
about 45 ml (3 Tbsp) avocado or olive oil
a good handful of roughly chopped
fresh coriander

1. Cook the pasta according to the packet instructions and allow to cool.
2. Add the rest of the ingredients and toss lightly. Serve at room temperature.

SERVES 4–6

Viv's Zingy Pink Lady

Inspired by a recipe from a dear friend, this is a pretty, summery salad, with a delicate balance between bittersweet and tart, and a fresh 'zingy' flavour. For a little extra sweetness, add a dash of good-quality balsamic reduction.

2 avocados, peeled and sliced
1 small lemon
2 ruby grapefruit, peeled and cut
into segments
1 cucumber, peeled and sliced into ribbons
60–80 g bean sprouts
30–45 ml (2–3 Tbsp) apricot oil
salt and black pepper to taste
8–10 sprigs fresh mint

1. Arrange the avocado slices on a plate in a fan shape. Squeeze fresh lemon juice over them.
2. Place a grapefruit segment between each slice of avocado and arrange the cucumber in a spiral over the top. Scatter over the bean sprouts, allowing them to 'tumble' over the cucumber.
3. Drizzle the apricot oil over the top, season with salt and pepper, and top with the mint.

SERVES 4

Pasta Salad

Mung Bean Soup

Butternut Soup

oil for frying
1 large onion, peeled and chopped
10 ml (2 tsp) crushed garlic
5 cm piece fresh ginger, finely chopped
1 large butternut, peeled, seeded and diced
2 large potatoes, peeled and cubed
2 vegetable stock cubes
2 litres (8 cups) water
125 ml (½ cup) fresh orange juice or
60 ml (¼ cup) soya cream

1. Heat the oil in a saucepan and fry the onion, garlic and ginger until softened.
2. Add the butternut, potatoes, stock cubes and water, and stir well.
3. Bring to the boil and cook for 15 minutes, then reduce the heat and allow to cook for 45 minutes on a medium to low heat. Top up with water if necessary; the soup must not be too thick.
4. Using a hand blender, blend the soup until smooth and silky, and allow to simmer for a further 5 minutes on a very low heat.
5. Stir in either the orange juice or soya cream, depending on preference. Allow to heat through and serve.

SERVES 4–6

Mung Bean Soup

500 ml (2 cups) mung beans, washed
1 litre (4 cups) water
45 ml (3 Tbsp) vegetable oil
5 ml (1 tsp) crushed garlic
1 onion, peeled and diced
1 chilli, chopped
2–3 sticks celery
2 carrots, peeled and chopped
750 ml (3 cups) vegetable stock
salt and black pepper to taste
250 ml (1 cup) finely diced cabbage (optional)
chopped fresh coriander (optional)

1. Bring the mung beans and water to the boil in a saucepan and simmer for about 45 minutes until the water is absorbed.
2. Heat the vegetable oil in a separate saucepan and sauté the garlic, onion, chilli, celery and carrots until slightly tender.
3. Add the mung beans and vegetable stock, and stir well.
4. Simmer for about 20 minutes, seasoning well with salt and pepper. If using, add the cabbage towards the end of the cooking process so that it retains its crunch.
5. Garnish with coriander if desired and serve with fresh crusty bread.

SERVES 3–4

Classic Vegetable Soup à la Lorne

This is truly heaven in a bowl and, as with most soups (and curries and stews), it tastes even better the next day. Make a huge pot and snack on it throughout the day.

2 large onions, peeled and diced
4 large cloves garlic, peeled and chopped
oil for frying
1 x 410 g can chopped peeled tomatoes
60 ml (¼ cup) tomato sauce
30 ml (2 Tbsp) tomato paste
15 ml (1 Tbsp) dried mixed herbs
5 ml (1 tsp) each of salt and black pepper
15 ml (1 Tbsp) ground ginger
15 ml (1 Tbsp) paprika
2 vegetable stock cubes, dissolved in
1.5–2 litres (6–8 cups) water
375 ml (1½ cups) soup mix (see page 164)
2 carrots, peeled and chopped
4 sticks celery, chopped (including leaves)
2 medium potatoes, peeled and cubed
2 leeks, cleaned and chopped
2 turnips, peeled and chopped
a large bunch of parsley, roughly chopped

1. In a large pot, fry the onion and garlic in oil until translucent.
2. Add the tomatoes, tomato sauce and tomato paste, and stir well.
3. Add the herbs, salt, pepper, ginger and paprika, and simmer for 10 minutes.
4. Add the remaining ingredients, except the parsley, and cook at a rolling boil, stirring frequently, for about 2 hours, adding more water if needed.
5. Sprinkle over the parsley just before serving with chunks of bread and a drizzle of olive oil.

SERVES 6–8

Lentil and Rice Salad

30 ml (2 Tbsp) balsamic vinegar
30 ml (2 Tbsp) fresh lime juice
60 ml (¼ cup) olive oil
5 ml (1 tsp) dried thyme
salt and black pepper to taste
500 ml (2 cups) cooked green lentils
250 ml (1 cup) cooked wild rice
6–8 spring onions, chopped
4 radishes, halved and thinly sliced
1 avocado, cubed

1. Whisk the balsamic vinegar, lime juice, olive oil, thyme, salt and pepper in a small bowl. Allow to stand for the flavours to develop.
2. Combine the lentils, rice, onions, radishes and avocado in a salad bowl. Stir gently, taking care not to crush the avocado.
3. Pour the dressing over the salad and serve with lime wedges and crusty garlic bread.

SERVES 4

The Sunday Soup

A tradition in our house is to make a big pot of hearty 'anything' soup on a Sunday afternoon, especially if the weather turns cold or rainy. It's an excellent way of using up whatever is hanging around in your fridge, getting sad and limp. Toss in veggies, beans and other odds and ends that are not enough for a meal by themselves. This soup improves with age, so make a lot of it and, whenever the children (anyone, actually) need a nourishing snack, a bowlful of soup will fill the gap.

60 ml (¼ cup) vegetable oil

1 onion, peeled and diced

as many garlic cloves as you like, peeled and chopped

15 ml (1 Tbsp) grated ginger

1 x 410 g can chopped peeled tomatoes

30 ml (2 Tbsp) tomato sauce or purée (if using purée add 5 ml/1 tsp sugar)

15 ml (1 Tbsp) dried mixed herbs

5 ml (1 tsp) paprika

2 litres (8 cups) vegetable stock or 1 litre vegetable stock + 1 litre chickpea stock

chopped veggies – whatever you have on hand that needs to be used – celery, carrots, cabbage, green beans, tomatoes, potatoes, turnips, courgettes and the like

leftover lentils, beans, split peas and barley

salt and black pepper to taste

roughly chopped fresh parsley or coriander to garnish

1. Heat the oil in a large pot and fry the onion, garlic and ginger until soft.
2. Add the tomatoes, tomato sauce or purée, herbs and paprika.
3. Simmer for 5–10 minutes.
4. Pour in the stock and add the chopped vegetables.
5. Rinse the pulses and add them to the soup mixture, stirring well. Rice or leftover bits of pasta can also be added directly to the soup, although add the pasta towards the end or it may become too soft.
6. Bring to the boil and cook for about 30 minutes, stirring regularly to prevent the pulses from sticking. Reduce the heat and simmer for about 2 hours until all the vegetables are soft and the pulses are cooked through.
7. Season with salt and pepper and sprinkle with parsley or coriander 5 minutes before serving.

SERVES 6–8

Spiced Lentil Soup

1 onion, peeled and chopped
5 ml (1 tsp) crushed garlic
oil for frying
5 ml (1 tsp) salt
5 ml (1 tsp) each of dried origanum and basil
2.5 ml (½ tsp) black pepper or to taste
5 ml (1 tsp) each of cumin, ground ginger and turmeric
1 x 410 g can chopped peeled tomatoes
30 ml (2 Tbsp) tomato sauce
2 vegetable stock cubes dissolved in 1 litre (4 cups) water *
125 ml (½ cup) each of red, brown (or black) and green lentils
125 ml (½ cup) green split peas**

1. In a large pot, fry the onion and garlic in oil until softened.
2. Add the salt, herbs, pepper, spices, tomatoes and tomato sauce, and simmer for 10–15 minutes.
3. Add the stock, followed by the lentils and split peas.
4. Bring to the boil, stirring frequently, for 1½–2 hours. Keep an eye on it, as the lentils tend to stick to the pot towards the end of the cooking process.
5. Serve warm, with chunks of fresh bread and a swirl of olive oil. A dash of vinegar stirred in rounds it off nicely.

SERVES 4–6

*Use 500 ml (2 cups) water and 500 ml (2 cups) ready-made chickpea stock (see page 8) for a richer, earthier flavour.
**250 ml (1 cup) frozen peas may be used instead; just add them in about 10 minutes before the end of cooking.

Marinated Mushroom and Vegetable Salad

MARINADE:
60 ml (¼ cup) olive oil
30 ml (2 Tbsp) fresh lemon juice
30 ml (2 Tbsp) apple cider vinegar
30 ml (2 Tbsp) chopped fresh parsley
5 ml (1 tsp) Dijon mustard
2.5 ml (½ tsp) salt
ground black pepper to taste

250 g button mushrooms, washed and sliced
oil for frying
1 carrot, peeled and julienned
1 red pepper, seeded and julienned
60 ml (¼ cup) olives
6–8 spring onions, chopped

1. Whisk the marinade ingredients together and leave to infuse.
2. Lightly fry the mushrooms in a little oil until just tender, and allow to cool.
3. Pour the marinade over the mushrooms, cover and chill in the fridge for about 1 hour.
4. Uncover and add the remaining ingredients, stirring well to combine the flavours.
5. Cover and return to the fridge for a further 1 hour. Bring to room temperature just before serving.

SERVES 4

Spiced Lentil Soup

Roasted Tomato Soup

Roasted Tomato Soup

1 kg ripe tomatoes, peeled and quartered
45 ml (3 Tbsp) olive oil
15 ml (1 Tbsp) chopped fresh origanum or
5 ml (1 tsp) dried
1 onion, peeled and chopped
5 ml (1 tsp) crushed garlic
5 ml (1 tsp) paprika
1 carrot, peeled and finely diced
2–3 sticks celery, chopped
10 ml (2 tsp) tomato paste
5 ml (1 tsp) sugar
1.5 litres (6 cups) vegetable stock made
with 2 stock cubes
2 bay leaves
olive oil or soya cream (optional)
chopped fresh parsley to garnish

1. Preheat the oven to 200 °C. Mix the tomatoes with the olive oil and origanum and roast for 30 minutes.
2. Fry the onion, garlic, paprika, carrot and celery for 10–15 minutes. Stir in the tomato paste and sugar, then add the roasted tomatoes and stir to combine.
3. Add the stock and bay leaves, and cook on a low heat for 20 minutes.
4. Remove the bay leaves and blend the soup with a hand blender or in a food processor.
5. Serve with a swirl of olive oil or soya cream and sprinkle with chopped fresh parsley.

SERVES 4–6

Classic Potato and Leek Soup

oil for frying
1 large onion, peeled and chopped
2–3 cloves garlic, peeled and chopped
3 large leeks, washed and chopped
5 ml (1 tsp) ground ginger
4–6 large potatoes, peeled and chopped
1 vegetable stock cube
2 bay leaves
1.5 litres (6 cups) water
250 ml (1 cup) soya milk*

1. Heat a little oil in a pot and fry the onion and garlic until soft.
2. Add the leeks and ginger, and fry for a further 5 minutes.
3. Add the remaining ingredients, except the milk, and bring to the boil. Reduce the heat and simmer for about 1 hour or until the potatoes disintegrate when skewered with a knife.
4. Remove from the heat and blend to the desired consistency – do half for a more chunky soup or the whole lot for a smoother, creamier version.
5. Return to a low heat, add the milk and simmer for 10 minutes. Serve with crusty bread.

SERVES 4–6

*For a creamier soup add 125 ml (½ cup) soya cream and 125 ml (½ cup) soya milk or omit the milk completely and add 250 ml (1 cup) soya cream.

Courgette and Lemon Soup

15 ml (1 Tbsp) vegetable oil
1 onion, peeled and finely diced
10 ml (2 tsp) crushed garlic
a thumb-size knob of ginger, grated
6 baby or 3 large courgettes, grated
1 litre (4 cups) vegetable stock
juice and zest of 1 lemon

1. Heat the oil in a pot and fry the onion, garlic and ginger until softened and aromatic.
2. Add the courgettes and stir well.
3. Pour in the vegetable stock and stir to combine.
4. Bring to the boil, then lower the heat and simmer for 30–40 minutes.
5. Right at the end of the cooking process, stir in the lemon juice.
6. Sprinkle the zest over the top just before serving with wedges of crusty, chunky homemade bread.

SERVES 4

Earthy Bean Soup

30 ml (2 Tbsp) vegetable oil
1 large onion, peeled and roughly chopped
4 cloves garlic, peeled and chopped
5 ml (1 tsp) salt
2 carrots, peeled and diced
3 fresh tomatoes, diced
30 ml (2 Tbsp) tomato sauce
500 ml (2 cups) chickpea stock or
1 litre (4 cups) vegetable stock made
with 1 vegetable stock cube
500 ml (2 cups) water
500 ml (2 cups) precooked kidney beans
salt and black pepper to taste
a handful of roughly chopped fresh parsley

1. Heat the oil in a pot and fry the onion and garlic until softened.
2. Add the salt, carrots, tomatoes and tomato sauce, and stir well. Pour in the stock and water, and bring to the boil.
3. Add the beans and stir well.
4. Reduce the heat and simmer for about 40 minutes. Season with salt and pepper, and add the parsley and more water if necessary. At this stage, the soup can be blended for a silkier, smoother version, or left chunky.
5. Serve with toasted pita-bread wedges or rustic wholewheat seed bread.

SERVES 4–6

Courgette and Lemon Soup

Corn and Coconut Chowder

Corn and Coconut Chowder

15ml (1 Tbsp) sunflower oil
1 onion, peeled and chopped
4–5 cloves garlic, peeled and chopped
500 ml (2 cups) vegetable stock
1 red pepper, seeded and diced
1 small chilli, seeded and diced
2 x 410 g can whole kernel corn
250 ml (1 cup) cooked haricot beans
500 ml (2 cups) soya milk
1 x 410 g can coconut cream
45 ml (3 Tbsp) chopped fresh parsley

1. Heat the oil in a saucepan, add the onion and garlic, and simmer for 10 minutes, until softened.
2. Add the remaining ingredients, except the coconut cream and parsley, and bring to the boil.
3. Reduce the heat and simmer for 15–20 minutes.
4. Add the coconut cream and parsley, and simmer for a further 5 minutes.

SERVES 4

French Chickpea Soup

500 ml (2 cups) dried chickpeas
2 litres (8 cups) cold water
1 onion, peeled and finely chopped
3–4 cloves garlic, peeled and chopped
5 ml (1 tsp) dried thyme
2–3 bay leaves
1 litre (4 cups) vegetable stock
5 ml (1 tsp) cumin
60 ml (¼ cup) olive oil
paprika to taste

1. Soak the chickpeas overnight in the cold water.
2. Drain and put into a large saucepan with the remaining ingredients, except the cumin, olive oil and paprika.
3. Simmer for 1–1½ hours until tender, then blend with a hand blender. Add more stock (or water) if necessary, but bear in mind the soup must be thick.
4. Add the cumin and simmer for a further 5–10 minutes.
5. Ladle into soup bowls, drizzle with the olive oil and sprinkle with paprika.

SERVES 4–6

Rustic Minestrone

60 ml (¼ cup) olive oil
1 onion, peeled and chopped
15 ml (1 Tbsp) chopped garlic
15 ml (1 Tbsp) grated ginger
3–4 sticks celery, chopped (reserve the leaves)
2 large carrots, peeled and chopped
1 x 410 g can chopped peeled tomatoes
15 ml (1 Tbsp) tomato paste
60 ml (¼ cup) tomato sauce
5 ml (1 tsp) each of dried origanum and basil
or 15 ml (1 Tbsp) each fresh
1.5–2 litres (6–8 cups) vegetable stock
250 ml (1 cup) cooked haricot beans
125 ml (½ cup) diced green beans
¼ cabbage, finely diced
250 ml (1 cup) broken spaghetti or macaroni
(or any bits of pasta you have to spare)
a big bunch of fresh parsley or
coriander, chopped
salt and black pepper to taste

1. Heat the oil in a pot and fry the onion, garlic, ginger, celery and carrots for 5–10 minutes.
2. Add the tomatoes, tomato paste, tomato sauce, herbs and stock, and bring to the boil. Simmer for 45 minutes, stirring every now and then, adding more water if necessary.
3. Add the remaining ingredients, including the reserved celery leaves, and simmer for a further 10–15 minutes.
4. Adjust seasoning and serve with chunks of crusty bread and a drizzle of olive oil.

SERVES 6–8

Main Meals

Bakes, pies, pizzas … who doesn't feel a pleasurable frisson at the thought of a good, hearty

home-cooked meal at the end of a long, hard day? A main meal can be a superbly satisfying soup, especially

in the cold months or on chilly days, or a rib-sticking, richly warming bake, stew, casserole or pie.

Not all bakes are meant for winter or the cold though: some are for comfort, some are for those days when

you are very hungry and only something steaming and filling will do. Some are pure indulgence,

like Dauphinoise, and provide something to look forward to when you feel like spoiling yourself.

And then there is Briam, which is something that everyone should eat, and often! Try it.

You will love every luscious, hearty mouthful.

When it comes to food, Italians know their stuff. Pasta is a staple in our house, eaten very often, and

in many forms. I have even been known to make my own which, while time consuming, is quite an adventure

and definitely worthwhile. Do try it sometime, but enlist the help of a willing participant!

But having said that, store-bought dried pasta is just as good. It's all about the sauce you make to complement

the pasta. At the end of the day, you can mix and match just about anything you have in your fridge or cupboard;

that's what it's all about, ultimately. Pasta was always a 'poor man's' dish – whatever was growing abundantly

in the garden went into the pot, along with whichever herbs were available (a very good reason to start your own

veggie patch). There was always a pot of something bubbling away, ready to feed a horde of hungry olive or grape

harvesters. Lashings of olive oil, a good rustic red and Voila!, dinner is served.

Dauphinoise (Rich Potato Bake)

Traditionally this dish oozes cheese and cream. We only omit the cheese; it is just as delicious and very, very rich. For an even more indulgent taste, substitute the soya milk for soya cream.

30 ml (2 Tbsp) sunflower or canola oil

2 onions, peeled and thinly sliced

15–30 ml (1–2 Tbsp) crushed garlic

salt and black pepper to taste

6 potatoes, peeled, parboiled and thinly sliced

250 ml (1 cup) soya cream mixed with

250 ml (1 cup) soya milk*

60 ml (¼ cup) mustard

250 ml (1 cup) toasted breadcrumbs

olive oil for drizzling

1. Preheat the oven to 160 °C. Coat the inside of a deep pie dish with the oil and spread half the onion and garlic in a layer at the bottom of the dish. Season with salt and pepper.
2. Cover with a layer of half of the potatoes. Pour half of the cream and milk mixture into the corner of the dish (so as not to disturb the seasoning).
3. Scatter the remaining onion and garlic over this, and layer the rest of the potatoes on top.
4. Pour the remaining cream and milk mixture into the dish.
5. In a small bowl, mix the mustard and breadcrumbs and spread liberally over the top of the potato.
6. Season well and drizzle with olive oil. Bake for 1 hour.

SERVES 4

*The amount may vary, depending on the size of your dish. A deeper bowl may need an extra 125 ml (½ cup). The liquid should almost cover the potatoes. For a slightly less rich dish, omit the cream and use only milk.

Lentil Bake

125 ml (½ cup) each of brown and green lentils

5 ml (1 tsp) vegetable oil

4 medium potatoes, peeled and sliced

2 onions, peeled and sliced

10–20 ml (2–4 tsp) crushed garlic

1 x 100 g pkt baby spinach leaves, steamed and excess liquid squeezed out

salt and black pepper to taste

10 ml (2 tsp) dried mixed herbs or 20 ml (4 tsp) fresh

500 ml (2 cups) vegetable stock

15 ml (1 Tbsp) paprika

60 ml (¼ cup) olive oil

1. Soak the lentils for 2–3 hours in fresh, cold water or boil for approximately 1 hour in a pot of boiling water.
2. Preheat the oven to 180 °C.
3. Grease a deep baking dish with the vegetable oil and layer the bottom with a third of the potato slices, half the lentils and then half the onions.
4. Sprinkle half of the garlic evenly over the onion slices, then spread the steamed spinach over this layer. Season with salt and pepper and half of the herbs. Repeat this process, ending with the last of the potato, and pour the vegetable stock over the top.
5. Season well with more salt and pepper and the remaining herbs, and sprinkle over the paprika. Drizzle with the olive oil and bake for 1 hour.

SERVES 4

Dauphinoise

Baked Tomatoes

Baked Tomatoes

30 ml (2 Tbsp) vegetable oil
1 onion, peeled and chopped
10 ml (2 tsp) crushed garlic
250 ml (1 cup) cooked brown or wild rice
5 ml (1 tsp) dried origanum
15 ml (1 Tbsp) chopped fresh parsley
6 tomatoes, halved and seeded*
45 ml (3 Tbsp) olive oil
125 ml (½ cup) toasted breadcrumbs
(optional)

1. Preheat the oven to 200 °C.
2. Heat the vegetable oil in a frying pan and sauté the onion and garlic until lightly golden.
3. Add the rice and continue sautéing until cooked through and lightly toasted. Add the herbs.
4. Place the tomato halves on a baking tray and fill each with the rice mixture. Drizzle over the olive oil. If using, sprinkle the breadcrumbs over for a crispy top.
5. Bake in the oven for 10–15 minutes until lightly browned and cooked through, but still firm. Serve with a fresh green salad and crusty bread.

SERVES 4

Briam

This is real 'peasant food'. You have to drink a rustic red wine with it. Oh, and it requires lashings of good olive oil, one of the few recipes that I would use extra-virgin olive oil to cook with. But don't skimp on this – it's worth every drop.

250 ml (1 cup) extra-virgin olive oil
1 kg potatoes, peeled and sliced into 0.5–1 cm-thick discs
2 large onions, peeled and sliced into rings
6 courgettes, sliced
5 tomatoes, peeled* and sliced
5 ml (1 tsp) each of salt and black pepper
15 ml (1 Tbsp) dried mixed herbs
10 cloves garlic, peeled and sliced
5 ml (1 tsp) each of ground ginger and paprika
750 ml (3 cups) vegetable stock
30 ml (2 Tbsp) tomato paste mixed with 50 ml hot water

1. Preheat the oven to 180 °C. Pour 15 ml (2 Tbsp) of the olive oil into a large casserole dish. Line the dish with half of the potato slices.
2. Layer all the sliced onion on top of the potatoes, followed by all the courgettes, then all the sliced tomato. Season with the salt and pepper, and half of the herbs.
3. Sprinkle over the garlic, ginger and paprika, and top with the remaining potato slices. Sprinkle over the remaining herbs and then gently pour the stock into the corner of the dish or over the top.
4. Pour over the tomato paste mixture and the remaining olive oil.
5. Bake for 1½ hours. Test the potatoes to see if they are done. A knife must slide through smoothly. If not, bake for a further 10–20 minutes.
6. Serve this with warm crusty bread to mop up the juices.

*To peel: cut a cross in the top and bottom of the tomatoes, then pour boiling water over them. When the skins start pulling back, remove from the hot water and place in cold water until cool to the touch. Peel off the skins.

SERVES 4

Spiced Butternut and Sweet Potato Tart

1 medium butternut, peeled, seeded and cubed

450–500 g sweet potato, peeled and cubed

60 ml (¼ cup) sunflower oil

2 red onions, peeled and cut into chunks

3–4 large cloves garlic, crushed

5 ml (1 tsp) paprika

2.5 ml (½ tsp) ground coriander

2.5 ml (½ tsp) ground cumin

2.5 ml (½ tsp) ground ginger

2.5 ml (½ tsp) cayenne pepper or to taste

5 medium tomatoes, roughly chopped into chunks

30 ml (2 Tbsp) olive oil

salt and black pepper to taste

1 x 400 g roll puff pastry

a little soya milk for brushing (optional)

1. Cook the cubed butternut and sweet potato in a pot of boiling water for 5–10 minutes until tender. Drain and set aside.
2. Preheat the oven to 200 °C.
3. Heat the sunflower oil in a heavy-bottomed ovenproof frying pan and fry the onions. Add the garlic and fry until softened.
4. Stir in the spices and add the tomatoes. Fry for 3–5 minutes until softened.
5. Add the butternut and sweet potato, and pour over the olive oil. Swirl around to make sure all the ingredients are evenly coated.
6. Season with salt and pepper.
7. Roll out the puff pastry to fit over the top of the pan and trim the edges to fit. Brush the top with a little soya milk (if desired), and bake for 30 minutes, until the pastry is golden brown.
8. This meal can either be served straight from the pan or inverted onto a plate, as you would an upside-down tart. Can be served with onion sauce (see page 149) or mushroom gravy (see page 158), a crisp fresh salad and chunky bread to mop up the juices.

SERVES 4

Butternut and Potato Bake

1 butternut, peeled and sliced

1 onion, peeled and sliced

4 medium potatoes, peeled and sliced

salt and black pepper to taste

45 ml (3 Tbsp) chopped fresh coriander

10 ml (2 tsp) dried origanum

500 ml (2 cups) vegetable stock

5 ml (1 tsp) ground ginger

10 ml (2 tsp) paprika

45 ml (3 Tbsp) olive oil

1. Preheat the oven to 180 °C.
2. Grease a large baking dish and layer half the butternut, half the onion and half the potato. Season well with salt and pepper, and sprinkle over the coriander and half the origanum.
3. Layer the rest of the butternut, onion and potato and pour over the stock.
4. Season again and sprinkle over the remaining origanum, as well as the ginger and paprika. Drizzle with the olive oil.
5. Cover with foil or the lid of the dish and bake for 50–60 minutes, until bubbling and cooked through.
6. Uncover and bake for a further 10–15 minutes or until the ginger and paprika have formed a crust and the top is a dark honey colour.

SERVES 4

Spiced Butternut and Sweet Potato Tart

Mushroom Pie

Mushroom Pie

15 ml (1 Tbsp) vegetable oil
350 g leeks, washed and sliced
10 ml (2 tsp) crushed garlic
1 onion, peeled and chopped
5 ml (1 tsp) ground coriander
500 g mushrooms, sliced
30 ml (2 Tbsp) cake flour
400 ml ale, such as Laurentina or Kilkenny
1 red pepper, seeded and chopped
15 ml (1 Tbsp) chopped fresh thyme or
5 ml (1 tsp) dried
125 ml (½ cup) soya cream
1 x 400 g roll puff pastry
soya milk for brushing

1. Preheat the oven to 180 °C.
2. Heat the oil in a saucepan and sauté the leeks, garlic, onion and coriander.
3. Add the mushrooms and fry until soft and tender. Sprinkle over the flour and stir well, then slowly add the ale. Add the red pepper and thyme.
4. Bring to the boil, then reduce the heat and simmer for 10 minutes.
5. Stir in the cream, remove the pan from the heat and set aside to cool slightly.
6. Roll out the pastry to 0.5 cm thick – there must be enough for a base and a top. Line a pie dish with half the pastry, so that it comes up the sides of the dish. Put another dish on top of the pastry or fill it with dried beans and bake blind for approximately 10 minutes.
7. Pour the mushroom mixture into the baked pastry case and cover with the remaining half of the pastry, tucking in the sides. Trim the edges and cut a cross in the centre to allow steam to escape. If there is any leftover pastry, make shapes to decorate the top of the pie.
8. Brush with soya milk and bake for 30 minutes or until the pastry is puffed and golden brown.

SERVES 4

Classic Cottage Pie

500 ml (2 cups) warm water
250 ml (1 cup) Nature's Choice soya mince
15 ml (1 Tbsp) vegetable oil
1 onion, peeled and chopped
10 ml (2 tsp) crushed garlic
2.5 cm-long piece ginger, grated
1 x 410 g can chopped peeled tomatoes
45 ml (3 Tbsp) tomato sauce
2 carrots, peeled and finely chopped
2 sticks celery, chopped
5 ml (1 tsp) dried sweet basil
3 medium potatoes, peeled and thinly sliced
15 ml (1 Tbsp) paprika
60 ml (¼ cup) olive oil

1. Pour the warm water over the soya mince and set aside for 20 minutes.
2. Preheat the oven to 180 °C.
3. Heat the vegetable oil a saucepan and fry the onion, garlic and ginger until soft.
4. Add the soya mince, tomatoes, tomato sauce, carrots, celery and basil, and season well with salt and black pepper. Cook on a medium heat for 30–40 minutes until the carrots are soft.
5. Pour the mixture into a pie dish and layer the sliced potatoes over the top, covering the filling. Sprinkle over the paprika and drizzle with the olive oil.
6. Bake for 40–50 minutes until the potatoes are cooked through. Serve with a fresh, crisp green salad.

SERVES 4

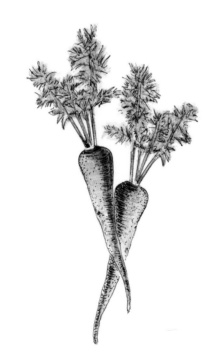

Lentil Cornish Pies

125 ml (½ cup) brown or black lentils
125 ml (½ cup) green lentils
15 ml (1 Tbsp) vegetable oil
1 onion, peeled and chopped
2 carrots, peeled and diced
5 ml (1 tsp) crushed garlic
2–3 chillies, chopped
125 g brown or white mushrooms, sliced
juice of ½ lemon
1 x 410 g can chopped peeled tomatoes or
5 fresh tomatoes, chopped
1 vegetable stock cube dissolved in
250 ml (1 cup) warm water
2 small potatoes, peeled and diced
5 ml (1 tsp) paprika
10 ml (2 tsp) soy sauce
45 ml (3 Tbsp) tomato sauce
80 ml (⅓ cup) frozen peas
1 x 400 g roll puff pastry
soya milk for brushing

1. Soak the lentils in cold, fresh water for 1 hour.
2. Preheat the oven to 180 °C.
3. Heat the vegetable oil in a saucepan and fry the onion, carrots, garlic and chillies until softened and aromatic.
4. Stir in the mushrooms and fry for a few minutes longer. Stir in the lemon juice, tomatoes and stock.
5. Add the lentils, potatoes, paprika, soy sauce and tomato sauce, and stir well. Add more water if the mixture seems too dry.
6. Bring to the boil, then reduce the heat and simmer for 45 minutes or until the lentils are cooked and most of the liquid is gone. Roughly 5–10 minutes before the end of cooking time, add the peas and heat through.
7. Roll out the puff pastry to about double the size and cut into four even rectangles. Place enough of the mixture on one half of each rectangle, while leaving a small border of about 2 cm. Fold the empty half over and crimp all around the edges with a fork to seal.
8. Make a small cross on the top of each pie and brush with a little soya milk. Place on a baking tray and bake for 30–40 minutes until golden brown on top.

SERVES 4

Pissaladière (French Onion Tart)

A tasty afternoon-into-evening meal that is very good for leftovers the next day, and makes an excellent finger food for when friends come round and no one wants to cook or eat a formal, sit-down meal.

DOUGH:
1 litre (4 cups) white bread flour
7.5 ml (½ Tbsp) salt
1 x 10 g sachet dry yeast
375–500 ml (1½–2 cups) tepid water

ONION TOPPING:
45 ml (3 Tbsp) olive oil
6 onions, peeled and sliced
10 ml (2 tsp) crushed garlic
15 ml (1 Tbsp) brown sugar
30 ml (2 Tbsp) balsamic vinegar
30 ml (2 Tbsp) chopped fresh thyme
salt and black pepper to taste
olive oil for drizzling
60 ml (¼ cup) pitted Calamata olives

1. To make the dough, mix the dry ingredients together and make a well in the centre. Add enough water to make a sticky dough and mix well.
2. Knead on a floured surface until smooth and elastic. Form into a ball and place the dough in an oiled bowl. Cover with clingfilm or a damp tea towel and leave to rise for 30 minutes.
3. Preheat the oven to 200 °C. Flour a rectangular baking tray.
4. Punch down the risen dough with your hands to flatten and then stretch or roll it out with a rolling pin to fit the baking tray.
5. Line the baking tray with the dough and dimple all over with your fingertips.
6. For the onion topping, heat the olive oil in a heavy-based frying pan and sauté the onions, garlic, sugar, balsamic vinegar and thyme.
7. After 10 minutes, lower the heat and leave the mixture to cook for 20–25 minutes, until nicely browned underneath, with a thick and syrupy relish- or marmalade-like consistency.
8. Spoon the mixture onto the dough, season with salt and pepper, and drizzle with olive oil. Spread the olives evenly over the top.
9. Bake for 20–25 minutes until the pastry crust is golden brown.

SERVES 4

Pot o' Chilli

This dish was inspired by a recipe I read a very long time ago, by someone who I imagine must have been an amazing lady to know, and whose passing was a sad loss to our earth – the late, great Linda McCartney.

30 ml (2 Tbsp) vegetable oil

1 large onion, peeled and chopped

10 ml (2 tsp) crushed garlic

2–3 chillies, diced

2.5 cm piece ginger, grated

2.5 ml (½ tsp) cayenne pepper

5 ml (1 tsp) ground cumin

5 ml (1 tsp) paprika

10 ml (2 tsp) dried origanum

1 x 410 g can chopped peeled tomatoes

60 ml (¼ cup) tomato sauce

15 ml (1 Tbsp) tomato paste

500 ml (2 cups) vegetable stock

375 ml (1½ cups) prepared red kidney beans or 1 x 410 g can kidney beans

salt and black pepper to taste

chopped fresh parsley to taste

freshly squeezed lemon or lime juice for serving

1. Heat the vegetable oil in a pot and fry the onion, garlic, chillies and ginger until softened. Add the spices, origanum, tomatoes, tomato sauce and tomato paste, and stir well.
2. Add the vegetable stock and kidney beans, and stir.
3. Bring to the boil, then reduce the heat and simmer for 30–40 minutes.
4. Just before serving, season well and stir in the parsley.
5. Dish up in deep bowls and squeeze fresh lemon or lime juice over the top. Serve with flat breads or tortilla chips to scoop up the chilli and, for extra zing, add some salsa (see below).

Salsa: Finely dice 2 tomatoes, 1 peeled onion and half a seeded green pepper. Stir together and season with salt and pepper. Squeeze in half a lemon and add a good drizzle of olive oil. You can add chopped fresh chilli if you desire.

SERVES 4

Vegetarian Bolognaise

250 ml (1 cup) Nature's Choice soya mince or
Fry's soya mince
15 ml (1 Tbsp) vegetable oil
1 onion, peeled and diced
10 ml (2 tsp) crushed garlic
2 carrots, peeled and finely chopped or grated
4 courgettes, finely chopped or grated
2 sticks celery, diced (including leaves)
1 x 410 g can chopped peeled tomatoes
60 ml (¼ cup) roast tomato sauce
(see page 148)
500 ml (2 cups) vegetable stock
20 ml (4 tsp) sugar
5 ml (1 tsp) each of dried origanum, basil
and parsley
5 ml (1 tsp) each of paprika and ground ginger
salt and black pepper to taste
chopped fresh parsley to taste

1. If using Nature's Choice, soak the soya mince in 500 ml (2 cups) warm water for 20 minutes to rehydrate. (Fry's mince is ready-made and does not need rehydrating.)
2. Meanwhile, heat the vegetable oil in a frying pan and fry the onion and garlic until lightly browned. Add the carrots, courgettes and celery, and fry for a further 10 minutes.
3. Add the tomatoes and tomato sauce, and stir well.
4. Add the mince and the remaining ingredients, except the fresh parsley, and stir well. Bring to the boil and cook for 10–15 minutes. Reduce the heat and simmer for approximately 45 minutes. Stir in the chopped fresh parsley during the last 5 minutes of cooking.
5. Spoon generously over cooked spaghetti.

SERVES 4

Variation: Use 250 ml (1 cup) green, brown or black lentils instead of soya mince, remembering to soak the lentils for a bit longer than the mince, up to 1 hour.

Pici

Pici is traditional, homemade pasta that does not contain any egg. It originates in Siena, Tuscany, and varies according to family tradition. It is hand-rolled and very much like spaghetti in appearance, except much fatter.

375 ml (1½ cups) white flour
125 ml (½ cup) chickpea flour
5 ml (1 tsp) salt
160 ml (⅔ cup) water
15 ml (1 Tbsp) olive oil

1. Mix the flours and salt together. Add the water and oil, and stir with a fork until the dough comes together.
2. Knead on a lightly floured surface until smooth and allow to stand for about 10 minutes, wrapped in clingfilm.
3. Divide the dough into 8 portions, keeping unused portions covered so that they don't dry out. Using a rolling pin, roll out one portion at a time on a floured surface until the desired thickness is achieved (2–3 mm is the norm). Alternatively, roll out in a pasta machine. Hang the sheets of pasta over anything suitable, such as the back of a chair, a clothes horse, etc.
4. Leave to rest for about 20 minutes before cutting. Either cut the pasta into thin ribbons for tagliatelle, linguine or fat pici, or into wider pieces for ravioli*. In the case of tagliatelle, cut into ribbons of the desired width and swirl handfuls into a sort of 'bird's nest', leaving to rest on a floured surface until ready to cook.
5. When ready, drop the pasta into salted, boiling water. Bring back to the boil and remove after 20 seconds. Drain and mix with whatever sauce you are using.

SERVES 4

* If you are making ravioli, lay the cut strip of pasta along a clean surface, such as a countertop, and place tablespoonfuls of your desired filling at regular intervals, about 5 cm apart. Place another strip the same width and length over them and cut through to form little parcels. Using a fork, press down the sides to seal in the filling. From there on, the cooking procedure is the same. For ravioli fillings, the choices are endless: spicy puréed butternut; mixed, fried mushrooms; hummus; mashed sweet potato; lentils and chilli; mashed peas; or even savoury soya mince.

Pici all'Aglione

Pici all'Aglione

60 ml (¼ cup) olive oil
2–3 chillies, diced
30 ml (2 Tbsp) crushed garlic
125 ml (½ cup) fine breadcrumbs
juice of ½ lemon
salt and black pepper to taste
1 quantity pici (see page 77), with some reserved cooking liquid
30 ml (2 Tbsp) chopped fresh parsley

1. Heat the olive oil in a heavy-based pan and fry the chillies and garlic until the garlic starts to brown.
2. Add the breadcrumbs and fry until golden brown and crisp.
3. Squeeze over the lemon juice, and season with salt and pepper.
4. Stir in the cooked pici with a little of the reserved cooking liquid.
5. Swirl together until the pici is well coated with the sauce. Sprinkle with the parsley before serving.

SERVES 4

Wok-fried Veggies

Thank you to Tammy Fry for sharing, and Debbie Fry for inventing, this tasty dish. Fry's products are quick and easy to prepare, so instead of a take-away, we always opt for something along these lines. Remember, when eating food prepared in a wok you can eat to your heart's content, because the veggies contain no fat and very little oil is used in the preparation. Veggies are only cooked for a short period of time, thereby maximising their nutritional value as they retain their vitamins and minerals.

1 x 300 g pkt Fry's vegetarian chunky strips
30 ml (2 Tbsp) sunflower oil
1 piece fresh root ginger, chopped
2 cloves garlic, crushed
2 red peppers, seeded and julienned
2 sticks celery, julienned
2 carrots, peeled and julienned
200 g mushrooms, sliced
2 spring onions, cut into rings
250 g cauliflower florets
200 g fresh bean sprouts
400 ml vegetable stock
90 ml (6 Tbsp) soy sauce
30 ml (2 Tbsp) cornflour
5 ml chopped fresh chilli
10 ml (2 tsp) lemon juice
freshly ground black pepper to taste

1. Fry the chunky strips in the oil in a wok over a high heat for about 6 minutes, until brown and crispy. Set aside and keep warm.
2. Briefly fry the ginger and garlic in the same wok – do not allow to burn. Add the vegetables and bean sprouts, and sauté for about 6 minutes, stirring continuously. The vegetables must remain crisp.
3. Stir together the stock, soy sauce and cornflour, and pour over the vegetables. Briefly bring to the boil, and season with chilli, lemon juice and black pepper.
4. Add the chunky strips back into the wok, stir and serve immediately.

SERVES 4

Spaghetti Genovese

300 g potatoes, peeled and roughly chopped
5 ml (1 tsp) salt
300 g spaghetti
200 g green beans, trimmed and halved
120 g pesto (see page 153)
salt and black pepper to taste
extra-virgin olive oil for drizzling
45 ml (3 Tbsp) chopped fresh parsley
or coriander

1. Bring a large pot of water to the boil, and add the potatoes and salt. Cook for 5 minutes until softened, then add the spaghetti and cook for a further 5 minutes or until almost tender.
2. Tip in the beans and cook for a further 5 minutes. Drain off the cooking liquid, reserving 60 ml (¼ cup).
3. Add the pesto and reserved liquid to the pot with the pasta and vegetables. Season well with salt and pepper, drizzle with olive oil and sprinkle over the fresh parsley or coriander.

SERVES 4

Rustic Roast Vegetables

4 medium carrots, peeled and cut into chunks
500 g baby potatoes (halve the larger ones)
2 onions, peeled and quartered
12 fat cloves garlic
1 green pepper, seeded and roughly chopped
2 fennel bulbs, quartered
2 lemons, halved
60 ml (¼ cup) olive oil
10 ml (2 tsp) coarse sea salt
5 ml (1 tsp) cracked black pepper
60 ml (¼ cup) balsamic vinegar
125 ml (½ cup) chopped fresh parsley

1. Preheat the oven to 200 °C.
2. Put all the ingredients, except the balsamic vinegar and parsley, into a roasting pan and mix well. Roast for 1–1½ hours, stirring and shaking every so often to prevent any vegetables from sticking.
3. Remove from the oven, drizzle with the balsamic vinegar and sprinkle over the parsley. Mix everything together to amalgamate the flavours and return to the oven for a further 15–20 minutes, until the balsamic has caramelised.
4. Serve spooned over crusty herb bread or stuffed in pita breads.

SERVES 4

Pecan Nut Gnocchi

I have a friend who has pecan nut trees on her farm, and when they fruit, they fruit. Bags and bags of these delicious, crunchy, darling little treasures fill whatever cupboard, fridge or freezer space is available. Nuts are a healthy and important part of a vegetarian diet, so spoil yourself as often as you like. Macadamia nuts are just as nice here, so mix and match.
Gnocchi is delicious served with any sauce, so experiment. A favourite of mine is arrabiata (see page 85). For those who can't handle the heat, a neapolitan sauce is just as good.

GNOCCHI:
1 kg potatoes
5 ml (1 tsp) salt
5 ml (1 tsp) white pepper (optional)
375 ml (1½ cups) white flour

PECAN NUT SAUCE:
125 ml (½ cup) chopped pecan (or macadamia) nuts
250 ml (1 cup) chopped fresh parsley (plus extra for garnishing)
45 ml (3 Tbsp) olive oil
15 ml (1 Tbsp) tomato paste
5 cloves fresh garlic, crushed
5 ml (1 tsp) salt

1. To make the gnocchi, cook the potatoes until very tender – you can steam, bake or boil them. While still hot, mash in a bowl with the salt and pepper, if using.
2. Slowly add the flour until you have a sticky, but manageable, dough. Knead on a lightly floured surface and shape into a rectangle about 1 cm thick.
3. Cut the rectangle into strips and roll the strips into 'ropes', about 1.5 cm in diameter. Cut the 'ropes' into 2 cm-long pieces. Place each piece on the inside bend of a fork and push down gently. This way, there is an indentation on the one side from your thumb and from the tines of the fork on the other. These ridges and indentations will help hold the sauce.
4. Place the gnocchi on floured baking trays, and refrigerate if not using immediately.
5. To cook, bring a large pot of salted water to the boil and drop in the gnocchi. They are cooked when they rise to the surface. Scoop them out with a slotted spoon and drain, reserving some of the cooking liquid.
6. To make the sauce, blend all the ingredients together with a little of the reserved cooking liquid from the gnocchi.
7. Add the gnocchi to the sauce and mix until well coated. Serve with fresh parsley sprinkled over the top.

SERVES 4

Our Classic Vegetable Lasagna

2 medium aubergines, sliced lengthways into
1 cm-thick strips and cross-hatched with a
sharp knife
125 ml (½ cup) olive oil
salt and black pepper to taste
15 ml (1 Tbsp) paprika
500 ml (2 cups) roast tomato sauce
(see page 148)
1 x 250 g box dried lasagne sheets (prepared
according to the instructions on the box)

BÉCHAMEL SAUCE:
60 ml (¼ cup) margarine
45 ml (3 Tbsp) cornflour
500 ml (2 cups) soya milk
30 ml (2 Tbsp) nutritional yeast
salt and black pepper to taste

1. Place the aubergine slices on a baking tray in a single layer and brush with 30 ml (2 Tbsp) of the olive oil. Season well with salt and pepper and sprinkle lightly with some of the paprika. Roast under a hot grill for about 10 minutes until slightly charred, but not burnt.
2. Preheat the oven to 180 °C.
3. Meanwhile, make the béchamel sauce. Melt the margarine in a saucepan and add the cornflour. Whisk continuously over a medium to high heat. As soon as the mixture starts to thicken, pour in the milk while still whisking. Add the yeast and stir. Season to taste.
4. Allow to bubble for 2–3 minutes, then remove from the heat.
5. Grease a large casserole dish with 30 ml (2 Tbsp) of the olive oil and spread 125 ml (½ cup) of the tomato sauce evenly on the bottom. Place one third of the lasagne sheets on top.
6. Spoon another 125 ml (½ cup) of the tomato sauce over the lasagne sheets. Top this with half of the grilled aubergine and cover with another 125 ml (½ cup) of the tomato sauce, still spreading evenly. Spread 250 ml (1 cup) of the béchamel sauce evenly over the tomato, and then cover with another one third of the lasagne sheets.
7. Spread the remaining 125 ml (½ cup) of the tomato sauce over the sheets, top this with the remaining aubergine and cover with the last of the lasagne sheets.
8. Spoon the remaining béchamel sauce over the lasagna sheets.
9. Drizzle the remaining olive oil over the top and sprinkle with the remaining paprika.
10. Bake for 45–60 minutes until the top is bubbling and crisp.

SERVES 6

Variation: For a more traditional lasagne, omit the aubergine and add 500 ml (2 cups) presoaked lentils or soya mince to the tomato sauce.

Arrabiata Pasta Sauce

1 large onion, peeled and chopped
4–5 cloves garlic, peeled and chopped
2–3 chillies, chopped
little oil for frying
3 medium tomatoes, peeled (optional) and
roughly chopped
1 x 410 g can chopped peeled tomatoes
60 ml (¼ cup) roast tomato sauce
(see page 148)
10 ml (2 tsp) sugar
15 ml (1 Tbsp) dried mixed Italian herbs (basil,
origanum, parsley)
5 ml (1 tsp) each of ground ginger and paprika
750 ml (3 cups) water
chopped fresh parsley to taste

1. Lightly fry the onion, garlic and chillies in a little oil until softened.
2. Add the tomatoes, canned tomatoes, tomato sauce, sugar, herbs and spices. Add 500 ml (2 cups) of the water and bring to the boil.
3. Boil for 15 minutes, then reduce the heat and simmer for up to 1 hour, adding extra water as needed. Add most of the chopped fresh parsley towards the end of cooking.
4. Serve spooned over cooked spaghetti with any remaining parsley sprinkled on top.

SERVES 4

Neapolitan Puttanesca

There is a fascinating tale behind the name Puttanesca, told to me years ago by a very dear lady of Italian heritage. Puttana is Italian for 'whore' and, while there are many different versions of the origin of the name of this dish, the most common is that in the 1950s, in the town of Naples, brothels were state owned and the 'inhabitants' of these houses of dubious distinction were only permitted to show their faces in the street for short bursts, and thus had to make do with hastily grabbed ingredients when doing their grocery shopping. Hence Puttanesca, or 'Whore's Pasta', which makes use of the most basic ingredients, but is ever present in all respectable Italian kitchens.

30 ml (2 Tbsp) vegetable oil
10 ml (2 tsp) chopped garlic
1 onion, peeled and chopped
2–3 chillies, diced
60 ml (¼ cup) chopped pitted black olives
30 ml (2 Tbsp) capers
4 tomatoes, peeled (optional) and chopped
30 ml (2 Tbsp) roast tomato sauce
(see page 148)
5 ml (1 tsp) dried origanum
5 ml (1 tsp) dried sweet basil
30 ml (2 Tbsp) chopped fresh parsley (plus
extra for garnishing)
salt and pepper to taste
oilve oil for drizzling

1. Heat the vegetable oil in a saucepan and sauté the garlic and onion. Add the chillies, olives, capers, tomatoes, tomato sauce and herbs.
2. Adjust seasoning and simmer for 30–40 minutes.
3. Stir in cooked and drained spaghetti and garnish with a good helping of chopped fresh parsley and a drizzle of olive oil.

SERVES 4

Macaroni Cheese

Macaroni Cheese

1 x 500 g pkt dried macaroni or whatever
pasta you fancy
60 ml (¼ cup) olive oil
1 quantity 'cheese' sauce (see page 153)
salt and black pepper to taste
3 medium tomatoes, sliced
1 onion, peeled and sliced into rings
5 ml (1 tsp) paprika

1. Preheat the oven to 180 °C.
2. Cook the macaroni according to the packet instructions. Drizzle a little of the olive oil into the base of a casserole dish and pour in the cooked pasta.
3. Pour over the 'cheese' sauce, retaining just over 125 ml (½ cup), and stir through until well mixed. Season with salt and pepper.
4. Arrange the sliced tomato and onion over the top and spoon over the rest of the 'cheese' sauce.
5. Drizzle over the remaining olive oil and sprinkle with the paprika.
6. Bake for 45 minutes or until bubbling and the paprika has formed a crispy crust.

SERVES 4

Spinach and Mushroom Ravioli

PASTA DOUGH:
1 ml (¼ tsp) salt
250 ml (1 cup) white bread flour
5 ml (1 tsp) olive oil
60 ml (¼ cup) water

FILLING:
1 x 200 g pkt baby spinach, washed
½ onion, peeled and chopped
3 cloves garlic, peeled and chopped
15 ml (1 Tbsp) olive oil
250 g button mushrooms, washed and sliced
5 ml (1 tsp) dried origanum
salt and black pepper to taste
250 ml (1 cup) roast tomato sauce
(see page 148)

1. To make the dough, stir the salt into the flour and make a well in the centre. Add the oil and water and knead well. The dough must be shiny and elastic. Allow the dough to rest for 1 hour.
2. Meanwhile, steam the spinach and set aside.
3. Fry the onion and garlic in the oil for 10 minutes.
4. Add the mushrooms and stir. Add the origanum, salt and pepper.
5. Cover and simmer until the mushrooms are tender and cooked through. Add the spinach and simmer for a further 10 minutes.
6. Roll out the dough, either with a pasta machine or a rolling pin. Cut into squares, about 7 x 7 cm.
7. Using a tablespoon, put a dollop of filling in the centre of each square. Cover with another square and push the sides together with a fork to enclose the filling.
8. Bring a large saucepan of water to the boil. Slowly add the ravioli and boil for 1½–2 minutes. Remove from the water with a slotted spoon and drain.
9. Heat the tomato sauce in a pan and add the ravioli, stirring until well coated with sauce. Serve on individual plates, with any leftover sauce spooned over the ravioli.

SERVES 4

Spaghetti alla Melanzane

This is a typically rustic, Italian country meal, made with fresh produce from the garden, handpicked on the day of making.

125 ml (½ cup) sunflower or canola oil
2 large aubergines, cubed
250 g dried spaghetti
60 ml (¼ cup) olive oil
1 large onion, peeled and diced
2 chillies, chopped
3 cloves garlic, peeled and chopped
60 ml (¼ cup) roughly chopped fresh thyme

1. Heat the sunflower or canola oil in a frying pan or shallow saucepan until quite hot. Add the aubergine cubes and fry, in batches if necessary, until golden brown. Drain on paper towel and set aside in a bowl.
2. Cook the pasta as per the packet instructions, coat with a little of the olive oil and set aside.
3. In the same pan used to fry the aubergine, heat about 30 ml (2 Tbsp) of the olive oil and fry the onion, chillies and garlic until softened and slightly browned.
4. Toss the cooked spaghetti into the pan with the other ingredients, add the crispy aubergine cubes and drizzle with the remaining olive oil. Sprinkle liberally with fresh thyme.
5. Serve warm and enjoy.

SERVES 4

Mushroom Lasagna

240 g (2 cups) mixed mushrooms, such as oyster, shiitake, brown, portobellini, washed and sliced
30 ml (2 Tbsp) olive oil
30 ml (2 Tbsp) chopped fresh thyme
1 quantity 'cheese' sauce (see pg 111)
1 x 250 g box lasagna sheets, prepared according to the instructions on the box
15 ml (1 Tbsp) olive oil
10 ml (2 tsp) paprika

1. Preheat the oven to 180 °C.
2. Fry the mushrooms in the oil until wilted and tender, and add the thyme.
3. Spoon one third of the 'cheese' sauce into the bottom of a casserole dish, then put a layer of the prepared lasagne sheets over the sauce.
4. Spoon half of the mushrooms over the lasagne sheets, then spoon over another third of the sauce.
5. Put down another layer of lasagne sheets and cover with the rest of the mushrooms.
6. Place another layer of lasagne over the mushrooms and spread the last of the sauce over the top.
7. Drizzle over the olive oil and sprinkle with the paprika.
8. Bake for 30 minutes.

SERVES 4

Spaghetti alla Melanzane

Breads

Bread is truly the staple of life. There are many ways of making bread, all of them deeply satisfying.

There are rustic farm-style breads, herb breads, vegetable breads, and let us not forget pizzas and focaccias,

which liven up any table. As well as Italian flat breads, there are Middle Eastern pitas, Indian chapatis and rotis,

and Mexican tortillas. Many wholewheat breads are made without any kneading involved, just a good, solid stir.

But there is enormous satisfaction in pummelling a ball of dough — ask any baker, or potter for that matter!

Mom's Pizza

I love pizza. To me it is 'lazy' food; put-your-feet-up-with-a-book-at-your-elbow sort of food. Not serious, sit-down-at-the-dinner-table-and-eat-with-a-knife-and-fork food, just a bite here, a bite there. A good pizza is juicy and crispy and, when finished, leaves a certain nostalgia and eager anticipation for the next one, with different toppings planned every time. That is the beauty of pizza – its versatility. Oh, and it always tastes excellent whether eaten hot or cold so, if you can, save some for tomorrow's lunchbox.

DOUGH:
1 litre (4 cups) white bread flour
10 ml (2 tsp) salt
1 x 10 g sachet dried yeast
375–500 ml (1½–2 cups) water
oil for rubbing

TOMATO BASE:
1 x 410 g can chopped peeled tomatoes
30 ml (2 Tbsp) tomato sauce
10 ml (2 tsp) sugar
5 ml (1 tsp) mixed dried Italian herbs
salt and black pepper to taste

chopped fresh herbs for garnishing
your choice of toppings: chilli, mushrooms, onion, peppers, garlic, artichokes, avocado, whatever else takes your fancy
olive oil for drizzling

1. Stir the flour, salt and yeast together in a bowl. Make a well in the centre and pour in most of the water, only adding the rest if necessary.
2. Mix well with a 'claw' hand until it all comes together.
3. Turn out onto a floured surface and knead well for about 5 minutes until smooth and shiny. Form into a ball and oil well. Put the dough in a bowl, cover with a damp tea towel or clingflim and allow to rise in a warm place for 1 hour.
4. Preheat the oven to 220 °C.
5. Blend together all the ingredients for the tomato base.
6. Knock back the dough and either stretch it into a circle to fit onto a large baking tray (or two medium trays) or roll it out with a rolling pin.
7. Spoon the tomato base over the surface, leaving a 1 cm border all around the edge. Sprinkle over some fresh herbs. Arrange your toppings evenly over the pizza, finishing with a drizzle of olive oil and some more herbs.
8. Bake for 20 minutes until the toppings are cooked through and the dough is golden and crispy.

MAKES 1 LARGE OR 2 MEDIUM PIZZAS

Note: For calzones, simply put the tomato base and toppings on one half of the pizza, fold over the other half and seal the edges.

Greek Vegetable Bread

1 litre (4 cups) white bread flour
5 ml (1 tsp) salt
1 x 10 g sachet dried yeast
375 ml (1½ cups) water
80 ml (⅓ cup) sundried tomatoes
10 ml (2 tsp) crushed garlic
60 ml (¼ cup) olive oil
salt and black pepper to taste
125 ml (½ cup) chopped fresh basil
125ml (½ cup) shredded fresh rocket
1 red pepper, roasted, peeled and cut
into strips

1. Combine the flour, salt and yeast in a bowl, make a well in the centre and add the water, stirring slowly to form a dough.
2. Knead on a floured surface and place in an oiled bowl. Cover and leave to rise in a warm place for 1 hour.
3. Knock back the dough and divide it into four equal balls. Take a ball of dough and roll it flat, about 1 cm thick, and place in a deep cake tin.
4. Place the sundried tomatoes and garlic onto the dough and drizzle with some of the olive oil. Season with salt and pepper.
5. Roll out another ball of dough and place it over the sundreid tomatoes and garlic. Layer this with the basil and rocket, drizzle over some more oil and season with salt and pepper.
6. Roll out the third ball and place over the basil and rocket. Layer this with the roasted red pepper, a drizzle of oil, and salt and pepper.
7. Roll out the remaining ball and place it over the red pepper layer. Drizzle with the remaining olive oil and season with salt and pepper.
8. Allow to stand for 1½ hours.
9. Preheat the oven to 200 °C and bake for 30 minutes.

SERVES 4–6

Note: Any combination of fillings may be used, such as olives, mushrooms, aubergines, pimentos, chillies, artichokes, etc.

Rosemary Focaccia

750 ml (3 cups) white bread flour
10 ml (2 tsp) salt
1 x 10 g sachet dried yeast
about 375 ml (1½ cups) water
a few sprigs fresh rosemary, chopped
3–4 cloves garlic, chopped
5 ml (1 tsp) coarse salt
45–60 ml (3–4 Tbsp) olive oil

1. Combine the dry ingredients in a bowl and make a well in the centre. Add enough water to make a sticky dough and mix well.
2. Knead the dough on a floured surface until smooth and elastic. Put into an oiled bowl, cover with clingfilm or a damp tea towel and leave for ½ hour.
3. Bash down the risen dough with your hands to flatten and then roll out with a rolling pin to fit a floured rectangular baking tray.
4. Stretch the sides of the dough to fit into the corners of the tray and dimple all over with your fingertips.
5. In a bowl, combine the rosemary, garlic, salt and olive oil, and stir well. Drop spoonfuls of the mixture onto the dough, spreading it with your fingers and making sure all the dimpled holes have some of the mixture pooling in them. Allow the bread to rest for ½ hour.
6. Preheat the oven to 200 °C and bake for 15 minutes or until golden.

MAKES 1 LARGE FOCACCIA

Chapatis

500 ml (2 cups) white bread flour
250 ml (1 cup) wholewheat flour
5 ml (1 tsp) salt
60 ml (¼ cup) sunflower oil
375 ml (1½ cups) water

1. Combine the flours and salt in a bowl and make a well in the centre.
2. Pour in the oil and water, and stir until the dough comes together. If you see it is going to be too dry, add a little more water, but not too much. If too sloppy, add a little extra flour.
3. Start kneading, making sure the dough is not too wet.
4. When you have a smooth and elastic consistency, wrap the dough in clingfilm and place in the fridge for about 30 minutes.
5. Divide the dough into equal portions: you should get about 8 medium or 10–12 small chapatis out of this amount.
6. Roll each portion out flat and stretch with your hands to about 12 cm in diameter for small chapatis or 18 cm for larger ones.
7. Heat a heavy-based frying pan (cast-iron is good, but not essential). Dry fry the chapatis for about 1 minute each side. They are done when there are small black 'singe' marks on either side. They must still be pliable, but not floppy.

MAKES 8 MEDIUM OR 10–12 SMALL

Cornbread

Cornbread

500 ml (2 cups) self-raising flour
10 ml (2 tsp) salt
10 ml (2 tsp) dried mixed herbs
1 x 400 g can corn
1 x 340 ml can beer or about 1 cup water

1. Preheat the oven to 180 °C. Grease and flour a bread tin.
2. Mix the flour, salt and herbs in a bowl and make a well in the centre.
3. Add the corn and beer or water, and stir until well mixed. The mixture should be slightly sloppy.
4. Pour into the bread tin and bake for 30–40 minutes until brown and crusty on top. Serve warm.

MAKES 1 LOAF

Turkish Flatbread

2.5 ml (½ tsp) each of coriander seeds and aniseeds
500 ml (2 cups) white bread flour
5 ml (1 tsp) salt
15 ml (1 Tbsp) chopped fresh coriander
160 ml (⅔ cup) warm water

1. Lightly toast the seeds in a dry frying pan and crush slightly in a mortar and pestle.
2. Combine the flour, salt, coriander and toasted seeds in a mixing bowl. Make a well in the centre and add the water. Mix together with the back of a wooden spoon until the dough comes together.
3. Knead the dough on a lightly floured surface until smooth. Form into a ball, cover with clingfilm and allow to stand for 30 minutes.
4. Divide the dough into 10 equal portions. Keep the ones not being rolled out in a bowl covered with a damp tea towel.
5. Roll out one portion to 10–15 cm in diameter and dry-fry in a non-stick frying pan over a high heat. This goes fairly quickly, taking only a few minutes. The flatbread must still be pliable and soft, with brown spots. Flip over and fry on the other side.
6. Repeat with the remaining portions of dough.

MAKES 10 FLATBREADS

Piadinas

750 ml (3 cups) white bread flour
5 ml (1 tsp) salt
3 ml (½ tsp) baking powder
45 ml (3 Tbsp) olive oil
200 ml (¾ cup) water

1. Mix the flour, salt and baking powder in a bowl. Make a well in the centre and pour in the oil and water. Mix with a 'claw' hand or a wooden spoon handle until the mixture comes together to form a dough.
2. Knead until smooth and shiny and wrap in clingfilm or cover with an upturned bowl. Leave to stand for ½ hour.
3. Divide the dough into 12 balls and roll out each one to a 15 cm-diameter, 5 mm-thick round.
4. Dry fry each one in a heavy-based frying pan for about 3 minutes each side or until evenly speckled with brown.

MAKES 12

Beer bread

500 ml (2 cups) cake flour
10 ml (2 tsp) bicarbonate of soda
10 ml (2 tsp) baking powder
5 ml (1 tsp) salt
1 x 340 ml can/bottle beer

1. Preheat the oven to 180 °C. Grease and flour a 20 cm round cake tin.
2. Combine all the dry ingredients in a bowl and stir. Make a well in the centre and add the beer, stirring until well combined.
3. Pour into the cake tin and bake for 45 minutes.

MAKES 1 LOAF

Piadinas

Cakes & Bakes

The aroma of a simple sponge cake wafting through a house can uplift and inspire even the most world-weary soul.

It has been said so many times, but baking truly is the epitome of all that is good and homely about a kitchen.

Just picture rich and spicy ginger cookies, those that zing and zest on your tongue, just like Moon-Face's 'pop

biscuits' in Enid Blyton's The Magic Faraway Tree. Or sweet and citrusy orange or apple cake with a spicy

cinnamon crust. Oh, and let's not forget delicately iced fairy cakes (for the children or the inner child) and the lush,

satisfying, decadent chocolate cake that hits the spot no matter the occasion (or lack thereof).

Vanilla-orange Fairy Cakes

500 ml (2 cups) cake flour
5 ml (1 tsp) bicarbonate of soda
10 ml (2 tsp) baking powder
2.5 ml (½ tsp) salt
125 ml (½ cup) sugar
125 ml (½ cup) vegetable oil
30 ml (2 Tbsp) grape vinegar
30 ml (2 Tbsp) vanilla essence
60 ml (¼ cup) fresh orange juice
250 ml (1 cup) water

VANILLA-ORANGE ICING:
125 ml (½ cup) soya butter
250 ml (1 cup) icing sugar
5 ml (1 tsp) vanilla essence
10 ml (2 Tbsp) orange juice
unwaxed orange zest for garnishing

1. Preheat the oven to 150 °C. Line a muffin pan with 12 cupcake papers.
2. In a large mixing bowl, combine the flour, bicarbonate of soda, baking powder, salt and sugar. Make a well in the centre.
3. Pour in the oil, vinegar, vanilla essence, orange juice and water. Swirl the wet ingredients around the bowl and slowly start to incorporate the dry ingredients until well combined. Take care not to overmix.
4. Spoon the mixture into the muffin pan and bake for 40 minutes until golden brown and cooked through. Test by inserting a knife or toothpick into the centre of a cupcake. If it comes out clean, the cupcakes are ready. Remove from the oven and set on a wire rack to cool.
5. To make the icing, cream the butter and sugar until light and fluffy. Stir in the vanilla essence and orange juice until the mixture comes together, using more or less orange juice to achieve a whipped-cream consistency. Chill the icing in the fridge.
6. Once the cupcakes have cooled, ice liberally and garnish with a twist of unwaxed orange zest for extra pizazz.

MAKES 12

Rayne's Orange Cake

The cinnamon crust used here is a favourite cake-decorating tip of mine. Not being partial to sweet, buttery icing, I always look for alternatives. This is an excellent one – the spicy cinnamon is perfectly offset by the sugar. There are two cakes that I especially favour the cinnamon crust with, and this is one of them. It's also my little boy's favourite cake.

500 ml (2 cups) cake flour
5 ml (1 tsp) bicarbonate of soda
10 ml (2 tsp) baking powder
2.5 ml (½ tsp) salt
125 ml (½ cup) sugar
125 ml (½ cup) olive oil
30 ml (2 Tbsp) vinegar
15 ml (1 Tbsp) vanilla essence
375 ml (1½ cups) fresh orange juice

CINNAMON CRUST:
30 ml (2 Tbsp) castor sugar
30 ml (2 Tbsp) ground cinnamon

1. Preheat the oven to 150 °C. Grease and flour a 20 cm round cake tin.
2. Stir the flour, bicarbonate of soda, baking powder, salt and sugar into a bowl. Make a well in the centre and add the remaining ingredients.
3. Mix thoroughly, making sure everything is combined, but do not overmix.
4. Pour the batter into the cake tin.
5. To make the crust, combine the sugar and cinnamon in a shaker and sprinkle all over the top of the cake, covering the entire surface.
6. Bake for 40–45 minutes. The cake is done when a knife inserted into the centre comes out clean.
7. Turn out onto a wire rack to cool.

Note: The cinnamon-sugar mixture is also perfect for pancakes.

Excellent Nutty Carrot Cake

375 ml (1½ cups) cake flour
5 ml (1 tsp) baking powder
5 ml (1 tsp) bicarbonate of soda
125 ml (½ cup) brown sugar
5 ml (1 tsp) salt
125 ml (½ cup) sunflower oil
15 ml (1 Tbsp) vinegar
15 ml (1 Tbsp) vanilla essence
250 ml (1 cup) cold water
2 carrots, peeled and grated
200 ml chopped pecan or macadamia nuts
60 ml (¼ cup) smooth apricot jam

1. Preheat the oven to 160 °C. Grease and flour a 20 cm cake tin.
2. Sift all the dry ingredients into a bowl and make a well in the centre. Add the wet ingredients, including the carrots and 125 ml (½ cup) of the nuts. Mix well.
3. Pour the batter into the cake tin and bake for 45 minutes. The cake is done when a knife inserted into the centre comes out clean.
4. Turn out onto a wire rack and allow to cool.
5. While still warm, brush the top with the apricot jam and sprinkle over the remaining nuts.

Gingerbread People

Children love to make and eat these, so let them do the kneading, decorating and even the cutting out — you may end up with some strange shapes, but they take such pride in their handiwork. Allspice is an important addition to this recipe; it just gives it that exotic edge.

500 ml (2 cups) cake flour
10 ml (2 tsp) baking powder
5 ml (1 tsp) salt
10 ml (2 tsp) ground ginger
5 ml (1 tsp) ground allspice
125 ml (½ cup) sugar
125 ml (½ cup) baking margarine, softened
60 ml (¼ cup) cold soya milk,
plus extra for basting
5 ml (1 tsp) molasses
raisins and cherries for decorating

1. Preheat the oven to 200 °C. Line a baking tray with baking paper.
2. Sift the flour, baking powder, salt, ginger, allspice and sugar into a large mixing bowl. Cut in the margarine and rub together using your hands.
3. Add the milk and molasses, and mix to form a dough.
4. On a floured surface, shape the dough into a ball. Roll it out to just less than 1 cm thick and cut out gingerbread people or whatever shapes the children desire. Continue until all the dough has been used.
5. Place the gingerbread people on the prepared baking tray and decorate with raisins for eyes and buttons, and cherries for mouths.
6. Bake for 15 minutes until golden brown. Allow to cool on a wire rack.

Banana Cake

250 ml (1 cup) wholewheat flour
250 ml (1 cup) cake flour
5 ml (1 tsp) bicarbonate of soda
10 ml (2 tsp) baking powder
5 ml (1 tsp) salt
60 ml (¼ cup) oil
125 ml (½ cup) sugar
60 ml (¼ cup) apple sauce
2 ripe bananas, peeled and mashed
5 ml (1 tsp) vanilla essence
125 ml (½ cup) water
icing sugar for dusting

1. Preheat the oven to 180 °C. Grease and flour a 20 cm cake tin.
2. Stir the flours, bicarbonate of soda, baking powder and salt into a bowl.
3. In a separate bowl or blender, whisk the oil and sugar together. Add the apple sauce and banana, and blend, ensuring there are no lumps.
4. Add this to the dry ingredients, mixing well until combined, but do not overmix.
5. Add the vanilla essence and, if necessary for consistency, the water. The batter should be thick, but just pourable.
6. Pour the batter into the cake tin and bake for 30 minutes or until a knife or skewer inserted into the centre comes out clean.
7. Turn out onto a wire rack and allow to cool before dusting lightly with icing sugar.

Classically Indulgent Chocolate Cake

375 ml (1½ cups) cake flour
45 ml (3 Tbsp) cocoa powder
30 ml (2 Tbsp) strong coffee granules
5 ml (1 tsp) bicarbonate of soda
5 ml (1 tsp) baking powder
80 ml (⅓ cup) sugar
5 ml (½ tsp) salt
1 ml (¼ tsp) cayenne pepper
80 ml (⅓ cup) sunflower oil
15 ml (1 Tbsp) vinegar
15 ml (1 Tbsp) vanilla essence
15 ml (1 Tbsp) molasses
250 ml (1 cup) cold water

CHOCOLATE ICING:
375 ml (1½ cups) icing sugar
30 ml (2 Tbsp) cocoa powder
15 ml (1 Tbsp) vanilla essence
30–45ml (2–3 Tbsp) hot water
icing sugar or glacé cherries for decoration

1. Preheat the oven to 150 °C. Grease and flour a 20 cm cake tin.
2. Sift the dry ingredients into a bowl and make a well in the centre.
3. Pour in the wet ingredients and slowly incorporate them without overmixing (but ensure there are no lumps).
4. Spoon the batter into the cake tin and bake for 45 minutes or until a skewer or knife inserted into the centre comes out clean.
5. Turn out onto a wire rack and allow to cool.
6. To make the icing, whisk together the ingredients until you have a smooth, lump-free mixture, the consistency of pouring cream.
7. Once the cake has cooled, pour the icing over the top, allowing it to cover the whole top of the cake and ooze down the sides. Decorate with a dusting of icing sugar or glacé cherries.

Note: This cake doubles as a coffee cake very successfully. Simply substitute the cocoa powder in both the cake batter and the icing with good-quality, strong coffee granules.

Chilli-chocolate Cake

It may sound a bit funny, but chilli and chocolate actually pair excellently. In countries like Mexico, where both chilli and chocolate are well-loved ingredients, the dishes that include these exotic and versatile ingredients are many and varied.

375 ml (1½ cups) cake flour
125 ml (½ cup) sugar
45 ml (3 Tbsp) cocoa powder
5 ml (1 tsp) baking powder
5 ml (1 tsp) bicarbonate of soda
7.5 ml (½ Tbsp) ground cinnamon
5 ml (1 tsp) cayenne pepper
15 ml (1 Tbsp) vanilla essence
15 ml (1 Tbsp) grape vinegar
80 ml (⅓ cup) sunflower oil
250 ml (1 cup) water
30–45 ml (2–3 Tbsp) icing sugar

1. Preheat the oven to 160 °C. Grease and flour a 20 cm round cake tin.
2. In a large bowl, stir together the flour, sugar, cocoa powder, baking powder, bicarbonate of soda and spices.
3. Make a well in the centre and add the vanilla essence, vinegar, oil and water. Stir until combined, but do not overmix.
4. Spoon the batter into the cake tin and bake for 40–45 minutes or until a knife inserted into the centre comes out clean.
5. Turn out onto a wire rack to cool before using a fine sieve to dust with the icing sugar.

Pomegranate Cake

Lemon Cake

This is a perfect summer cake to serve on a sultry afternoon with a snappy, crisp white wine or ice-cold lemonade.

500 ml (2 cups) cake flour
5 ml (1 tsp) bicarbonate of soda
10 ml (2 tsp) baking powder
2.5 ml (½ tsp) salt
125 ml (½ cup) sugar
125 ml (½ cup) vegetable oil
15 ml (1 Tbsp) vinegar
60 ml (¼ cup) lemon juice
250 ml (1 cup) cold water

LEMON ICING:
juice of 1 lemon
sifted icing sugar
lemon zest for decoration

1. Preheat the oven to 150 °C. Grease and flour a 20 cm cake tin.
2. Sift the dry ingredients into a bowl and make a well in the centre.
3. Add the wet ingredients and mix well, but do not overmix.
4. Pour the batter into the cake tin and bake for 40–45 minutes or until a skewer or knife inserted into the centre comes out clean.
5. Turn out onto a wire rack and allow to cool.
6. To make the lemon icing, squeeze the lemon juice into a bowl and slowly add icing sugar, stirring well to break up any lumps, until the mixture has the consistency of thick cream.
7. Spread the icing over the top of the cooled cake and decorate with shavings of lemon zest.

Pomegranate Cake

375 ml (1½ cups) cake flour
5 ml (1 tsp) baking powder
5 ml (1 tsp) bicarbonate of soda
1 ml (¼ tsp) salt
15 ml (1 Tbsp) grape vinegar
15 ml (1 Tbsp) vanilla essence
60 ml (¼ cup) sunflower oil
125 ml (½ cup) sugar
250 ml (1 cup) pomegranate juice
seeds of ½ pomegranate
juice of 1 orange
5 ml (1 tsp) poppy seeds
5 ml (1 tsp) castor sugar

1. Preheat the oven to 180 °C. Grease and flour a 20 cm square cake tin.
2. Stir together the flour, baking powder, bicarbonate of soda and salt.
3. Make a well in the centre and add the vinegar, vanilla essence, oil, sugar and pomegranate juice. Mix well.
4. Pour the batter into the cake tin and bake for 35–40 minutes or until a knife inserted into the centre comes out clean.
5. Turn out onto a wire rack to cool.
6. Once the cake has cooled, put the pomegranate seeds, orange juice, poppy seeds and castor sugar in a small saucepan and bring to the boil, stirring constantly.
7. Allow to thicken and pour over the cooled cake, letting the orange glaze ooze down the sides.

Nutty Spiced Banana Muffins

250 ml (1 cup) wholewheat flour
250 ml (1 cup) cake flour
2.5 ml (½ tsp) salt
5 ml (1 tsp) baking powder
5 ml (1 tsp) bicarbonate of soda
5 ml (1 tsp) each of paprika and ground ginger
125 ml (½ cup) chopped pecan nuts or almonds or any nut of your choice
3 ripe bananas, peeled and mashed
125 ml (½ cup) sugar
250 ml (1 cup) soya milk
80 ml (⅓ cup) sunflower oil

1. Preheat the oven to 180 °C. Grease a muffin pan.
2. Sift the flours, salt, baking powder, bicarbonate of soda and spices into a bowl. Stir in the nuts.
3. In a separate bowl or blender, blend the bananas, sugar, milk and oil together until smooth.
4. Add this to the dry ingredients and mix well until moist.
5. Spoon the mixture into the muffin pan, filling each hole to about three-quarters of the way up the sides. Top with a mixture of chopped nuts, brown sugar and soya butter if desired.
6. Bake for 20 minutes. Turn out of the pan and allow to cool on a rack.

MAKES 12

Easy-peasy Scones

Scones have never been easier. This recipe is completely flop-proof. Once you've made it once or twice, you can experiment with adding sweet goodies such as cherries, chocolate chips and nuts; or savoury goodies such as dried apricot bits, sun-dried tomatoes and olives.

500 ml (2 cups) cake flour
10 ml (2 tsp) baking powder
5 ml (1 tsp) bicarbonate of soda
10 ml (2 tsp) castor sugar
15 ml (1 Tbsp) butter
250 ml (1 cup) soya milk, plus extra for basting

1. Preheat the oven to 240 °C. Lightly grease a 24 cm square baking tray.
2. Combine the flour, baking powder, bicarbonate of soda and sugar.
3. Rub in the butter using your fingertips. Make a well in the centre and add almost all of the milk, stirring to form a soft, sticky dough. Add the rest of the milk if the dough is too dry.
4. Knead the dough on a lightly floured surface, but don't over knead; just make sure the consistency is even.
5. Roll out to a thickness of about 2 cm, dip a round cutter or glass into a little flour and cut as many rounds as you can from the dough.
6. Place the scones on the baking tray so that they are just touching.
7. Brush the tops with a little soya milk and bake for 10–15 minutes, or until the tops of the scones are golden brown and they sound hollow when tapped underneath.
8. Eat warm, with lashings of apricot jam.

MAKES 10

Apple Cake with Cinnamon Crust

This is delicious served with a little preserved ginger on the side or perhaps a swirl of soya cream.
The classic combination of apple and cinnamon never disappoints.

450 ml cake flour
5 ml (1 tsp) bicarbonate of soda
10 ml (2 tsp) baking powder
2.5 ml (½ tsp) salt
125 ml (½ cup) sugar
125 ml (½ cup) sunflower oil
250 ml (1 cup) apple juice
15 ml (1 Tbsp) vinegar
15 ml (1 Tbsp) vanilla essence

CINNAMON CRUST:
30 ml (2 Tbsp) castor sugar
30 ml (2 Tbsp) ground cinnamon

1. Preheat the oven to 150 °C. Grease and line a 20 cm cake tin.
2. Sift the flour, bicarbonate of soda, baking powder, salt and sugar into a mixing bowl.
3. Make a well in the centre and pour in the wet ingredients, and mix until combined.
4. Pour the batter into the cake tin and shake a little to even out.
5. Mix the castor sugar and cinnamon and sprinkle this over the top, ensuring the cake is well covered. Pay special attention to the edges. Add more if necessary – the cake mix must not be visible.
6. Bake for 40–45 minutes until the cinnamon-sugar has formed a hard crust.

Treacle Cake

500 ml (2 cups) cake flour
5 ml (1 tsp) bicarbonate of soda
10 ml (2 tsp) baking powder
2.5 ml (½ tsp) salt
125 ml (½ cup) treacle sugar
125 ml (½ cup) sunflower oil
30 ml (2 Tbsp) grape vinegar
30 ml (2 Tbsp) vanilla essence
15 ml (1 Tbsp) treacle or molasses
60 ml (¼ cup) warm water
250 ml (1 cup) tepid water

CHOCOLATE ICING:
125 ml (½ cup) soya butter, softened
250 ml (1 cup) icing sugar
15 ml (1 Tbsp) cocoa powder
30 ml (2 Tbsp) vanilla essence

1. Preheat the oven to 150 °C. Grease and flour a 20 cm round cake tin.
2. Combine the dry ingredients in a large mixing bowl.
3. Make a well in the centre and add the oil, vinegar and vanilla essence.
4. Stir the treacle or molasses into the warm water until dissolved and add this to the mixture.
5. Add the tepid water and mix well, making sure all the components are combined.
6. Pour the batter into the prepared cake tin and bake on the middle shelf of the oven for 40–45 minutes. The cake is done when a knife inserted into the centre comes out clean. Turn the cake out onto a wire rack to cool.
7. To make the icing, cream the butter and sugar until light and fluffy. Stir in the cocoa powder and vanilla essence. Chill in the fridge.
8. When the cake and icing are completely cooled, ice the cake.

Rustic Apricot Biscuits

250 g (1¼ cups) cake flour
5 ml (1 tsp) baking powder
2.5 ml (½ tsp) salt
125 ml (½ cup) treacle sugar
15 ml (1 Tbsp) vinegar
150 g (1¼ cups) soya butter, softened
30 ml (2 Tbsp) milk
30–45 ml (2–3 Tbsp) apricot jam

1. Preheat the oven to 160 °C. Either grease and flour or line a 24 cm square baking tray with baking paper.
2. Combine the dry ingredients, then add the vinegar, butter and milk.
3. Cut through the butter with a blunt knife until the mixture becomes crumbly. Start kneading until the dough comes together, adding a little extra milk if necessary. When the dough has been well kneaded and is an even colour, break off pieces the size of R5 coins and roll into balls.
4. Place the balls on the baking tray and flatten a little with a wet fork (dip the fork into warm water now and then to prevent sticking). The flattened balls must be about 2 cm high.
5. Using either your finger or the back of a wooden spoon, make a hole in the top of each biscuit, about 1 cm deep. Be careful not to go all the way through. Spoon about a 2.5 ml (½ tsp) of the apricot jam into each cavity.
6. Bake for 15–20 minutes. Remove from the oven and cool on a wire rack.

MAKES ABOUT 22

Crumbly Cookies

250 g (1¾ cups) cake flour
115 g (½ cup) sugar
5 ml (1 tsp) baking powder
1 ml (¼ tsp) salt
115 g (½ cup) soya butter
60 ml (¼ cup) soya milk
15 ml (1 Tbsp) vanilla essence
15 ml (1 Tbsp) vinegar

1. Preheat the oven to 160 °C. Either grease and flour or line a 24 cm square baking tray with baking paper.
2. Combine the dry ingredients in a mixing bowl.
3. Cut in the butter and rub the mixture between your fingertips to incorporate.
4. Pour in the milk, vanilla essence and vinegar.
5. Stir well with a wooden spoon, then start to pick up handfuls of the dough, squeezing it in your fists until it all comes together. If the mixture remains very crumbly, add a little more milk, up to 15 ml (1 Tbsp). Knead the dough until well amalgamated.
6. Break off small pieces, about the size of R5 coins and place them on the baking tray, leaving 2 cm gaps between them.
7. Dip a fork in water and squash the balls, but not too flat or they will break up.
8. Bake for 15–20 minutes. Turn out onto a wire rack to cool.

MAKES ABOUT 20

Note: These darlings can be dipped into melted chocolate and sandwiched together for a special treat. Children love to help with the rolling, so let them!

Desserts & Sweets

Once again, the Italians say it best – La Dolce Vita (the sweet life). There are some tempting tasties here,

for the very sweet and the not-so-sweet tooth. I do not have much of a sweet tooth at all, but I have to say

that now and then a decadent, tempting treat hits the spot.

A plus of not eating dairy is that food contains much less fat. So you can enjoy sorbet and gelato all the more!

Oh, and don't skimp on the (dairy-free) chocolate: 100 percent dark chocolate with a hint of mint

or perhaps a twist of orange zest…

Almond Panforte

Traditionally, panforte is made with honey, hazelnuts and dried figs. This is my version and is just as good.
A drop or two of rum or brandy will jazz this up into an adult after-dinner treat.

80 g dark chocolate
60 ml (¼ cup) vegetable oil
80 ml (⅓ cup) castor sugar
80 ml (⅓ cup) golden syrup
45 ml (3 Tbsp) cocoa powder
160 ml (⅔ cup) cake flour
5 ml (1 tsp) ground cinnamon
1 ml (¼ tsp) each of ground nutmeg and
ground coriander
150 g (1 cup) chopped raw almonds
or walnuts
150 g (1 cup) chopped dried apricots
30–45ml (2–3 Tbsp) rum or brandy (optional)
icing sugar for dusting

1. Preheat the oven to 180 °C. Grease a baking tray.
2. Melt the chocolate with the oil, sugar and syrup in a double boiler or in a bowl over a pot of hot water on the stove.
3. Combine the cocoa powder, flour, spices, nuts and apricots in a bowl, and fold into the chocolate. If using, add the rum or brandy. Mix well to combine. If the mixture is too dry, add a little extra oil. If too sloppy, add a little extra flour.
4. Roll into small balls and place on the baking tray. Press gently to flatten and bake for approximately 10 minutes.
5. Remove from the baking tray and allow to cool before dusting liberally with sifted icing sugar. These can be stored for up to 2 weeks in an airtight container.

SERVES 4

Upside-down Apple Tart

Dairy-free Chocolate Fridge Tart

There is a slight deviation from tradition here. Most fridge tarts have a biscuit-butter base with the chocolate mix poured over the top.
This recipe requires the biscuits, butter and chocolate to be mixed together.

230 g (1 cup) margarine

250 ml (1 cup) soya or coconut cream

80 g (⅔ cup) roughly chopped dairy-free dark chocolate

120 g (1 cup) crushed ginger biscuits

75 g (½ cup) chopped pecan nuts, cashews or almonds (or a mixture)

1. Melt the margarine, cream and chocolate in a double boiler over a low heat.
2. Stir in the biscuits and nuts.
3. Line a springform cake tin with greaseproof paper and pour in the mixture, shaking gently to ensure even distribution. Give the sides a gentle tap to release any trapped air bubbles.
4. Refrigerate for 2–3 hours until set.
5. Serve with dairy-free ice cream or fresh fruit.

SERVES 4

Upside-down Apple Tart

410 ml (1⅔ cups) cake flour

5 ml (1 tsp) ground cinnamon

2.5 ml (½ tsp) ground nutmeg

5 ml (1 tsp) ground ginger

5 ml (1 tsp) baking powder

5 ml (1 tsp) bicarbonate of soda

1 ml (¼ tsp) salt

125 ml (½ cup) chopped pecan nuts

125 ml (½ cup) soya butter, softened

125 ml (½ cup) sunflower oil or 200 ml apple sauce

200 ml treacle sugar

15 ml (1 Tbsp) grape vinegar

2 medium Pink Lady apples or any apples of your choice, peeled, cored and thinly sliced (1 cm thick)

1. Preheat the oven to 170 °C. Grease and flour a 20 cm round cake tin.
2. In a bowl, mix the flour, cinnamon, nutmeg, ginger, baking powder, bicarbonate of soda and salt. Add the nuts, if using.
3. In a separate bowl, cream the butter, oil or apple sauce, sugar and vinegar. Slowly pour this into the flour mixture, incorporating the two, but taking care not to overmix.
4. In the bottom of the prepared cake tin, layer the apple slices. Then spread the batter evenly over the apples.
5. Bake for 30–35 minutes, or until the cake is firm and a knife inserted into the centre comes out clean.
5. Allow the cake to cool completely in the tin, before sliding a knife all around the edge and inverting it onto a plate to serve.

Unforgettable Chocolate Ice Cream

Very rich and creamy with an exotic flair, this is an excellent alternative to dairy ice cream. For a less full-bodied flavour, omit the coconut cream and use more soya or coconut milk. For variation, use vanilla instead of cocoa, or chocolate chips instead of nuts (or as well as). You can even add broken-up honeycomb (the type you get in Cadbury's Crunchie® bars). This ice cream is also excellent in a Dom Pedro.

1 x 400 ml can coconut cream
1 x 400 ml can coconut milk
250 ml (1 cup) soya milk
125 ml (½ cup) sugar
45 ml (3 Tbsp) cocoa powder
45 ml (3 Tbsp) coffee granules
125 ml (½ cup) chopped pecan nuts
or almonds

1. In a large mixing bowl, combine all the ingredients, except the nuts, and blend with a hand blender until the cocoa and coffee have dissolved.
2. Stir in the nuts, then pour the mixture into a freezer-friendly container and freeze for 5–6 hours or overnight.
4. Remove from the freezer about 15 minutes before serving, to allow the ice cream to soften a little.

SERVES 4

Ginger Shortbread

These are creamy, crumbly and taste like home. If ginger isn't your thing, you can just leave it out.

375 ml (1½ cups) cake flour
15 ml (1 Tbsp) ground ginger
80 ml (⅓ cup) castor sugar plus an extra
30 ml (2 Tbsp) for dusting
125 ml (½ cup) soya butter, softened
30 g (¼ cup) chopped macadamia or pecan
nuts (optional)

1. Preheat the oven to 150 °C.
2. Stir the flour and ginger together, then add the sugar.
3. Cut the butter into the flour and rub together with your fingers.
4. When you have a crumbly texture, start to squeeze parts of the mixture together in your fists, incorporating more and more until all of the mixture has come together.
5. Place on a clean surface and knead, slowly integrating the chopped nuts, if using.
6. Press the dough out into a 20 cm, ungreased baking tray and lightly score, without cutting all the way through, how big you would like your biscuits to be. If you are using a round tray, cut segments as you would a cake, but for a square or rectangular tray you can cut either fingers or squares.
7. Decorate the segments by pricking with a fork, especially on the edges.
8. Bake for 30 minutes.
9. Remove from the oven and cut the segments all the way through. Dust with the extra castor sugar and allow to cool, but do not remove from the tray. When completely cool, store in an airtight container.

MAKES 12–16

Strawberry Granita

Strawberry Granita

Granita is very similar to sorbet, the only real difference being that granita is usually more textured, with chunkier, less-refined ice crystals.

120 g blackberries, raspberries or
strawberries (or a mixture)
100 g sugar
juice of ½ lemon
400 ml water
15 ml (1 Tbsp) vodka (optional)

1. Whizz the berries in a blender and then pass through a sieve to remove any seeds or lumpy bits.
2. Add the sugar and stir well until dissolved.
3. Add the lemon juice and water, and stir well. Add the vodka, if using.
4. Pour the mixture into a flat, freezer-friendly container and freeze until crystallised, stirring intermittently with a fork to break up any lumps.

SERVES 4

Note: This recipe can also be used to make pomegranate granita. Simply omit the berries and use fresh pomegranate juice. Remember that anything frozen becomes less sweet, so add sugar accordingly.

Traditional Crumpets

750 ml (3 cups) cake flour
15 ml (1 Tbsp) castor sugar
5 ml (1 tsp) salt
1 x 10 g sachet dried yeast
375 ml (1½ cups) water
375 ml (1½ cups) soya milk
30 ml (2 Tbsp) vegetable oil

1. Blend the flour, sugar, salt, yeast, water and milk in a bowl and leave to stand for 1 hour.
2. Heat some of the oil in a heavy-bottomed frying pan and drop spoonfuls of the mixture into the pan.
3. When the surface of a crumpet is full of fine holes and sponge-like in appearance, turn it over and cook on the other side. Repeat until all the batter is used, oiling the pan whenever necessary.
4. Serve warm with dairy-free ice cream or whipped cream, such as Orley Whip, and drizzled with maple syrup.

MAKES 10–12

Boozy Mango Pots

1 mango, peeled and cubed
juice of 1 lime
juice of 1 granadilla
5 ml (1 tsp) sugar
10 ml (2 tsp) orange liqueur (optional)
60 ml (¼ cup) non-dairy whipped cream (such as Orley Whip)
pips of 1 granadilla

1. Place the mango, lime juice, granadilla juice and sugar into a blender and blend until smooth and creamy.
2. Stir in the liqueur (if using) and cream.
3. Serve in small dessert glasses with a spoon or thin wafer biscuits, topped with the granadilla pips.

SERVES 2

Note: Brandy works just as well if orange liqueur is not available.

Apple Crumble

4–5 apples, peeled and chopped
125 ml (½ cup) seedless raisins
250 ml (1 cup) orange juice (preferably freshly squeezed)
10 ml (2 tsp) brown sugar
1 cinnamon stick

CRUMBLE:
125 ml (½ cup) oats
10 ml (2 tsp) sunflower seeds
10 ml (2 tsp) chopped almonds or pecan nuts
10 ml (2 tsp) brown sugar

1. Preheat the oven to 180 °C.
2. Bring the apples, raisins, orange juice, sugar and cinnamon to the boil in a saucepan.
3. Turn down the heat and simmer for about 10 minutes until tender.
4. Meanwhile, combine the crumble ingredients, rubbing them together with your hands.
5. Remove the cinnamon stick from the apple mixture and spoon the contents of the saucepan into a pie dish.
6. Evenly sprinkle the crumble over the apples and bake for 10–15 minutes until golden and bubbling.

SERVES 6–8

Boozy Mango Pots

My Bread and Butter Pudding

30 ml (2 Tbsp) margarine
60 ml (¼ cup) apricot jam
6 traditional hot-cross buns, halved

CUSTARD:
1 litre (4 cups) soya milk
60 ml (¼ cup) custard powder
60 ml (¼ cup) sugar
45 ml (3 Tbsp) vanilla essence

1. Preheat the oven to 180 °C.
2. To make the custard, heat 250 ml (1 cup) of the milk in a saucepan. Slowly whisk in the custard powder and sugar, whisking constantly until the custard starts to thicken. Take care here, because once it does thicken, it goes quite fast. Slowly pour in the remainder of the milk and stir in the vanilla essence. Taste and add a little more sugar if necessary.
3. Spread the margarine, followed by the jam, onto the cut side of each hot-cross bun half. Close the buns.
4. Pour a little of the custard into a baking dish, ensuring the base of the dish is covered. Fit the hot-cross buns into the dish.
5. Pour over the remaining custard, making sure all the buns are covered. Allow to stand for about 15 minutes.
6. Bake for about 20 minutes until golden brown and bubbling. Serve warm.

SERVES 6

Cheat's Crêpe Suzette

500 ml (2 cups) cake flour
30 ml (2 Tbsp) sunflower oil
30 ml (2 Tbsp) castor sugar
750 ml (3 cups) soya milk

SAUCE:
80 ml (⅓ cup) margarine
45 ml (3 Tbsp) castor sugar
juice and zest of 1 orange
juice of ½ lemon
15 ml (1 Tbsp) sugar
30 ml (2 Tbsp) brandy
30 ml (2 Tbsp) orange liqueur

icing sugar and ground cinnamon for dusting
soya cream for serving

1. Blend the flour, oil, sugar and milk, and refrigerate for 30 minutes.
2. Pour 80 ml (⅓ cup) of the batter into a heated, non-stick frying pan. Cook for 2–3 minutes or until bubbles form on the top and the sides become lacy and frothy. Turn over the pancake and cook the other side. Set the finished pancake aside and keep warm while you make the rest.
3. For the sauce, melt the margarine, 30 ml (2 Tbsp) of the castor sugar and the orange zest and juice in a non-stick frying pan.
4. Roll the pancakes into cigars and slice as you would a Swiss Roll.
5. Stir the pancake strips into the orange mixture and squeeze over the lemon juice.
6. Add the remaining castor sugar, along with the sugar, brandy and orange liqueur, and swirl until warmed through.
7. Serve warm with a dusting of icing sugar and ground cinnamon, and a dollop of soya cream on the side.

SERVES 4

My Bread and Butter Pudding

Bub's Apricot Tart

1 x 400 g roll shortcrust pastry
125 ml (½ cup) smooth apricot jam
125 ml (½ cup) chopped pecan nuts
30 ml (2 Tbsp) desiccated coconut
15 ml (1 Tbsp) soya milk

1. Preheat the oven to 180 °C.
2. Divide the pastry in half and roll out each half to fit a 20 cm pie dish.
3. Use one half to line the dish, trimming the edges to fit and making sure they are not too high up the sides of the dish, about 3 cm is fine. Prick holes in the base with a fork and bake blind for 10 minutes.
4. Remove from the oven and spread with the jam. Sprinkle over the nuts and coconut.
5. Cover with the other piece of pastry and trim the edges to fit. Using a fork, join the two pieces of pastry all around the edges. Alternatively, make a lattice top by cutting the pastry into strips and criss-crossing them over the filling.
6. Decorate the top of the pie by cutting out small diamond shapes from the leftover bits of pastry. Prick here and there with a fork, baste with the soya milk and bake for 20 minutes or until golden brown.
7. Allow to cool before serving with soya cream or ice cream.

SERVES 6–8

Banana Sorbet

As with granita (see page 131), sorbets can have any number of different flavours. Try making them with apple, pear or peach juice.

3 ripe bananas, peeled
250 ml (1 cup) sugar
45 ml (3 Tbsp) lemon juice
60 ml (¼ cup) vodka (optional)
500 ml (2 cups) water
500 ml (2 cups) fresh orange juice
fresh mint leaves for garnishing

1. Blend the bananas, sugar, lemon juice and vodka (if using) in a blender.
2. Put the mixture into a steel bowl, Tupperware® or any freezer-proof hard-plastic container and stir in the water and orange juice.
3. Place in the freezer to set, scraping the crystals away from the sides of the bowl every 30 minutes. When semi-frozen all the way through, serve in cocktail glasses and garnish with mint leaves.

SERVES 4

Note: Plain banana can also be made into an excellent 'ice cream' all by itself. Simply cut a banana into chunks, freeze and blend until the consistency is smooth and creamy. Stir in a teaspoon or two of vanilla essence and you have a creamy, tasty dessert.

Drinks

A very important part of eating, and enjoying eating, are the drinks chosen to go with the meal.

And by that I don't mean red wine with this or white wine with that; red wine goes with just about anything

as far as I am concerned! But who doesn't enjoy an ice-cold glass of homemade lemonade on a hot day or a jug

of fruity, zesty sangria on a long, lazy afternoon? And let's not forget the warm comfort of rich and foamy hot

chocolate when the weather becomes rainy and windy, and the nights turn cold. Not to mention the Irish coffees…

Homemade Lemonade

500 ml (2 cups) water
250 ml (1 cup) sugar
juice of 7–8 unwaxed lemons
500 ml (2 cups) sparkling water
fresh mint leaves for garnishing

1. Bring the water to the boil in a saucepan and add the sugar. Stir until the sugar has dissolved, then remove from the heat and allow to cool.
2. Add the lemon juice to the cooled sugar water and stir well.
3. Pour into a jug, add the sparkling water and chill in the fridge.
4. Serve with ice and garnished with mint leaves.

MAKES 4 CUPS (1 LITRE)

Iced Tea

1 litre (4 cups) water
4 rooibos tea bags
60 ml (¼ cup) sugar
15 ml (1 Tbsp) fresh lemon juice
lemon slices and sprigs of fresh mint for garnishing

1. Bring the water to the boil in a saucepan. Add the tea bags and sugar, and boil for about 20 minutes.
2. Turn off the heat and allow the mixture to infuse until cool. Taste before the water has cooled completely, and add more sugar if necessary.
3. Add the lemon juice and stir.
4. Serve with lots of ice and garnished with slices of lemon and sprigs of mint.

MAKES 4 CUPS (1 LITRE)

Sangria

1 x 750 ml bottle red wine
250 ml (1 cup) fresh orange juice
250 ml (1 cup) store-bought or homemade lemonade (see above)
2 apples, peeled, cored and diced
2 slices fresh pineapple, chopped
zest of 2 lemons, cut into thin strips
3–4 lemon slices, halved

1. Combine all the ingredients in a jug and refrigerate until ice cold.

MAKES 4¼ CUPS (1.25 LITRES)

Homemade Lemonade

Whiskey Sours

Whiskey Sours

A classic from a bygone era, this is to be savoured slowly.

45 ml (3 Tbsp) fresh lemon juice
80 ml (⅓ cup) whiskey
500 ml (2 cups) crushed ice
a few sprigs of fresh mint for garnishing

1. Blitz the lemon juice, whiskey and ice in a blender until slushy.
2. Pour into two martini glasses and serve with a short straw and a few sprigs of mint.

SERVES 2

Limoncello

This is a treat drunk all over Southern Italy, and you will find variations of it in every region, each family swearing that theirs is best. It is often poured over granita or gelato as an after-dinner treat, but is just as good on its own. This recipe has two stages that span four weeks, so make it in advance!

8 unwaxed lemons
750 ml (3 cups) vodka
500 ml (2 cups) spring water
210 g (1 cup) castor sugar
60 ml (¼ cup) whole fresh mint leaves

1. Soak the lemons in a bowl of cold water for 1 hour. With a vegetable peeler, peel the lemon rind, taking care to leave the bitter pith behind. Reserve the lemons for use in something like lemonade (see page 140).
2. Place the lemon rind in a jar and cover with the vodka. Leave to stand in a dark place for 3 weeks.
3. After 3 weeks, place the water, sugar and mint leaves in a saucepan and bring to the boil. Once the sugar has dissolved, remove from the heat, cover and allow to cool.
4. Once the mixture has cooled, add the lemon rind and vodka. Strain and decant into sterilised, dry bottles and seal. Leave to stand in a cold, dark place for 1 week.
5. Serve ice cold, and refrigerate after opening.

MAKES 1 LITRE (4 CUPS)

Ginger Beer

Brisk and refreshing, nothing beats homemade ginger beer. A shot of rum or vodka turns this into a feisty afternoon splash.

500 ml (2 cups) water
350 g ginger root, peeled and grated
80 ml (⅓ cup) sugar
10 unwaxed limes or 8 lemons
OR 3 limes and 5 lemons
soda water and ice for serving

1. Bring the water to the boil in a saucepan and stir in the ginger and sugar, until the sugar has dissolved. Remove from the heat and leave to cool completely. Strain.
2. Squeeze the limes and/or lemons, and add the juice to the cooled mixture (heat kills Vitamin C, which is why the water must be cool before adding the juice).
3. Refrigerate and serve ice cold, topped up with soda water and ice to the required concentration.

MAKES 750 ML (3 CUPS)

Hot Chocolate

Just like the real thing!

500 ml (2 cups) soya milk
1 ml (¼ tsp) cayenne pepper
1 cinnamon stick
80 g good-quality, non-dairy dark chocolate
cocoa powder for dusting

1. Heat the milk in a saucepan (do not boil). Add the cayenne pepper and cinnamon, and allow to infuse. Crumble in the chocolate and swirl until melted.
2. Serve warm with a light dusting of cocoa powder and shortbread biscuits to dip.

SERVES 1

Hot Chocolate

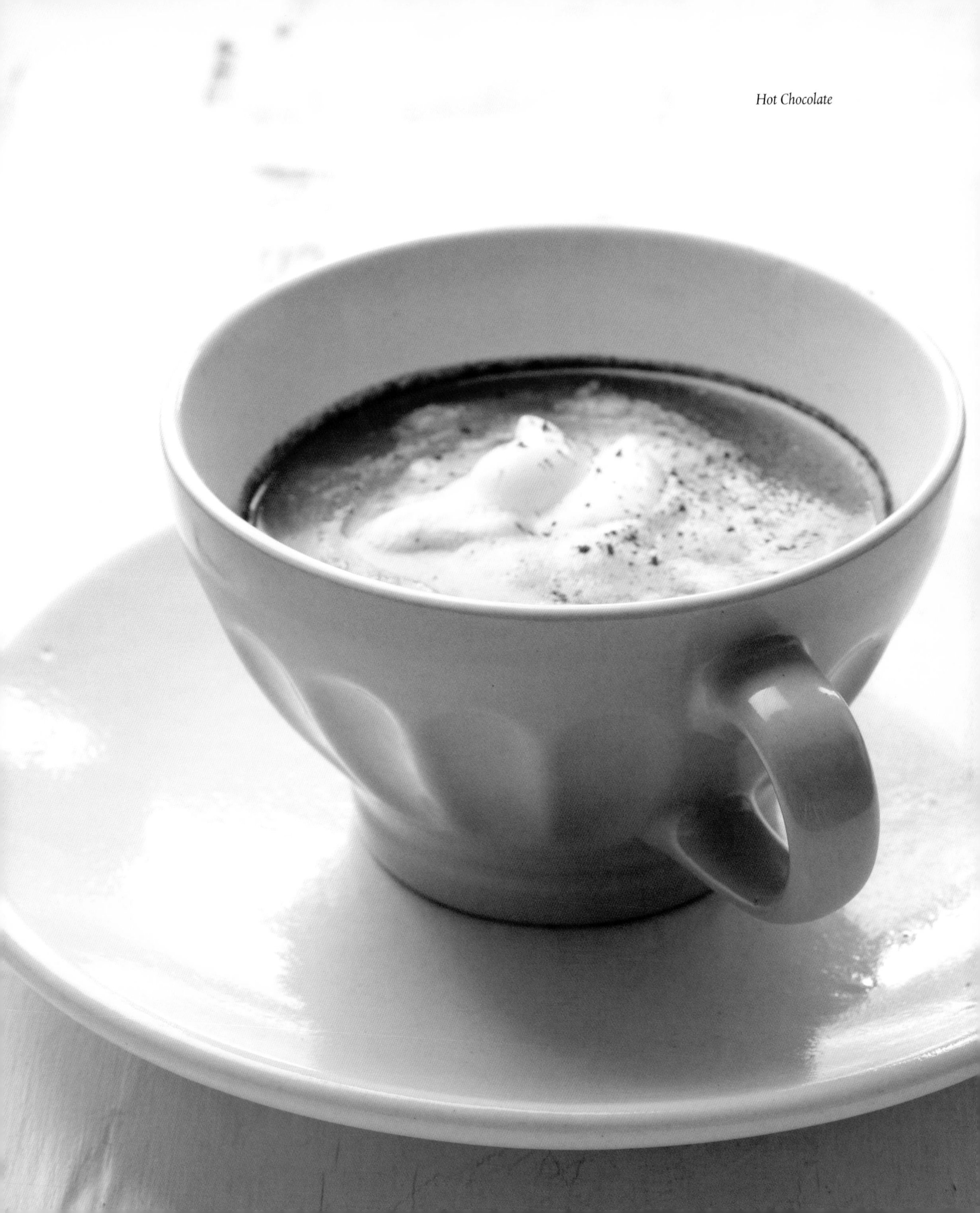

Sauces, Spreads & Dips

These are the things that make the world go round. You can't have snacks without a dip or sauce.

And what would samosas be without a chilli sauce or spring rolls without a sweet and sour sauce?

My absolute favourite, and the one I am quite famous for (if I say so myself), is hummus. It's versatile and

totally delicious on just about anything, and kids absolutely love it. It's also very healthy. We have a tradition

in our family – whenever we go camping, we make hummus sandwiches for the car and whatever is left gets

put into a grid and then put on the braai that night, to eat for breakfast or lunch the following day.

Sort of like toasted hummus sandwiches. Delicious!

Roast Tomato Sauce

I use this sauce as a base for absolutely everything. It freezes really well, so make extra for those days when you need a sauce and don't feel up to cooking one – just whip up some spaghetti, add a chopped fresh chilli, a handful of capers and some leftover cooking liquid and you have a quick, healthy meal on the table in no time. Use in lasagne, as a soup base or as gravy for pies – the options are endless. Note that the sauce is quite concentrated.

5–6 fresh tomatoes, quartered
3–4 cloves garlic, crushed
10 ml (2 tsp) dried origanum
10 ml (2 tsp) dried sweet basil
60 ml (¼ cup) olive oil
5 ml (1 tsp) sugar
5 ml (1 tsp) salt
5 ml (1 tsp) cracked black pepper

1. Preheat the oven to 220 °C.
2. Place the tomatoes, garlic and herbs in a roasting pan. Drizzle over 30 ml (2 Tbsp) of the oil and bake, uncovered, for 20–30 minutes, until the tomatoes are soft.
3. Purée the tomatoes with the remaining ingredients in a blender. The sauce can be fine or chunky, depending on preference.

MAKES 250 ML (1 CUP)

Sweet and Sour Sauce

250 ml (1 cup) white grape vinegar
60 ml (¼ cup) castor sugar
30 ml (2 Tbsp) lemon juice
30 ml (2 Tbsp) roast tomato sauce
(see above)

1. Bring all the ingredients to the boil in a saucepan.
2. Allow time to infuse, about 10 minutes, then reduce the heat and simmer for 20 minutes or until the sauce starts to thicken. Stir occasionally.
3. Remove from the heat and allow to cool.
4. Use as a dipping sauce for spring rolls or samosas, in stir-fries, etc.

MAKES 250 ML (1 CUP)

Note: For a sweet and sour chilli sauce (sublimely delicious), simply add 2–3 finely chopped chillies.

Onion Sauce

15 ml (1 Tbsp) sunflower oil
2 onions, peeled and chopped
15 ml (1 Tbsp) cornflour stirred into
30 ml (2 Tbsp) soya milk
80 ml (⅓ cup) soya milk
160 ml (⅔ cup) vegetable stock
15 ml (1 Tbsp) chopped fresh thyme

1. Heat the oil in a frying pan and fry the onion until softened.
2. Stir in the cornflour mixture and slowly whisk in the milk and stock. Add the thyme and simmer until the sauce thickens.
3. Use as a gravy for roast potatoes, mushroom pies or Yorkshire puddings.

MAKES 310–375 ML (1¼–1½ CUPS)

Hummus

1 x 400 g can chickpeas or
375 ml (1½ cups) prepared chickpeas
¼ onion, peeled and roughly chopped
juice of 1 lemon
10 ml (2 Tbsp) vinegar
45 ml (3 Tbsp) olive oil
10 ml (2 tsp) salt
2.5 ml (½ tsp) crushed garlic, or to taste
cracked black pepper to taste
30 ml (2 Tbsp) chopped fresh parsley
5 ml (1 tsp) paprika
extra olive oil for drizzling

1. Whizz all the ingredients, except the paprika and extra oil, in a blender on high speed until the desired consistency is achieved.
2. Add more oil or lemon juice to taste or to thin the volume out a bit.
3. Transfer to a dish, dust the paprika over the top and drizzle over a light layer of olive oil for a deep, jewelled red hummus.
4. Serve with fresh, homemade bread, pitas or chapatis.

MAKES 250 ML (1 CUP)

Homemade Chilli Sauce

1 x 410 g can chopped peeled tomatoes
5 ml (1 tsp) each of dried origanum, basil and parsley
5 ml (1 tsp) paprika
15 ml (1 Tbsp) roast tomato sauce (see page 148)
15 ml (1 Tbsp) crushed garlic
30 ml (2 Tbsp) balsamic vinegar
30 ml (2 Tbsp) olive oil
30 ml (2 Tbsp) lemon juice
5 ml (1 tsp) salt
2.5 ml (½ tsp) sugar
5–6 fresh chillies, roughly chopped

1. Bring the tomatoes, herbs, paprika, tomato sauce and garlic to the boil in a saucepan, stirring constantly.
2. Reduce the heat, cover and simmer gently for about 30 minutes, until thick and viscous. Remove from the heat and allow to cool.
3. Blend the tomato mix with the remaining ingredients. The amount of blending will depend on whether you want a smooth or chunky sauce.
4. Spoon into sterilised, dry jars and pour a layer of olive oil over the top to seal. Keep refrigerated and use within 3–4 weeks.

MAKES 250 ML (1 CUP)

Basic Béchamel Sauce

60 ml (¼ cup) soya margarine
45 ml (3 Tbsp) cornflour
500 ml (2 cups) soya milk
30 ml (2 Tbsp) nutritional yeast
2–3 whole bay leaves
5 ml (1 tsp) garlic or onion salt
freshly ground black pepper to taste

1. Melt the margarine in a saucepan over a medium to high heat. Add the cornflour and whisk continuously. As soon as the mixture starts to thicken, pour in the milk while still whisking.
2. Add the yeast, bay leaves, salt and pepper, and stir.
3. Allow to bubble for 2–3 minutes, before removing from the heat.
4. Remove the bay leaves before using.

MAKES 250 ML (1 CUP)

Homemade Chilli Sauce

'Cheese' Sauce

'Cheese' Sauce

60 ml (¼ cup) soya margarine
45 ml (3 Tbsp) cornflour
500 ml (2 cups) soya milk
30 ml (2 Tbsp) nutritional yeast
2–3 whole bay leaves
5 ml (1 tsp) garlic or onion salt
freshly ground black pepper to taste
15 ml (1 Tbsp) Dijon mustard or
5 ml (1 tsp) mustard powder
5 ml (1 tsp) turmeric

1. Melt the margarine in a saucepan over a medium to high heat. Add the cornflour and whisk continuously. As soon as the mixture starts to thicken, pour in the milk while still whisking.
2. Add the yeast, bay leaves, salt, pepper, mustard and turmeric, and stir well until combined.
3. Allow to bubble for 5 minutes, before removing from the heat.
4. Remove the bay leaves before using.

MAKES 250 ML (1 CUP)

Pesto

750 ml (3 cups) chopped fresh basil or parsley
80 ml (⅓ cup) sunflower or sesame seeds
5 large cloves garlic, peeled and roughly chopped
5 ml (1 tsp) sea salt
60 ml (¼ cup) olive oil
15 ml (1 Tbsp) fresh lemon juice (optional)
60 ml (¼ cup) pine nuts (optional)

1. Blend all the ingredients in a blender until smooth and creamy. For a little extra zing, add the lemon juice. For a more traditional twist, add the pine nuts.
2. Use as a pasta sauce or in baked, stuffed mushrooms.

MAKES 125 ML (½ CUP)

Gremolata

10 ml (2 tsp) crushed garlic
juice and zest of 1 lemon
60 ml (¼ cup) chopped fresh parsley
30 ml (2 Tbsp) toasted breadcrumbs
45 ml (3 Tbsp) olive oil
salt and black pepper to taste

1. Whisk all the ingredients together in a bowl.
2. Adjust the seasoning and toss with freshly cooked pasta, spoon over a potato salad or mix into roast vegetables.

MAKES 60 ML (¼ CUP)

Marula Jelly

Abundant in the Lowveld and packed with Vitamin C, marulas are a delicious alternative to oranges. A true Slowvelder (thanks Jackie!) recipe, this jelly is reminiscent of honey and is heavenly on a piece of hot toast, or as an accompaniment to roast veggies.

2.5 kg marula fruit (use half green and half ripe fruit, as the green fruit contains more pectin, which helps in the gelling process)
6 cups white sugar
juice of 2 lemons

1. Wash the marulas and cut or pierce the skins. Place in a large saucepan, cover with water and boil for 15–20 minutes.
2. Strain the liquid through a cloth (muslin or cheesecloth) into a large clean saucepan.
3. Add sugar at a ratio of 1:1, so for every cup of marula juice add 1 cup of sugar. Heat gently, stirring to dissolve the sugar.
4. Add the lemon juice and bring to the boil for 20 minutes or until gelling temperature has been reached. To check this, pour a teaspoon of the mixture onto a cold saucer and allow to cool. Push gently with your finger and if the jelly wrinkles, it is ready.
5. Place the marula jelly into sterilised jars and allow to cool. Seal and store in a cool place. Refrigerate once opened.

MAKES 2 LITRES (8 CUPS)

Gremolata

Aubergine Pâté

Aubergine Pâté (Baba Ghanoush)

3 aubergines, halved and cross-hatched
5–6 cloves garlic, peeled
80 ml (⅓ cup) olive oil
5 ml (1 tsp) ground cumin
5 ml (1 tsp) paprika
juice of 1 lemon
salt and black pepper to taste
chopped fresh parsley for garnishing

1. Preheat the oven to 150 °C.
2. Place the aubergines and garlic in a roasting pan and drizzle with about 45 ml (3 Tbsp) of the olive oil. Roast for about 45 minutes until tender.
3. Allow to cool and scoop out the aubergine flesh, discarding the skins.
4. Purée all the ingredients, except the parsley, in a blender or mash with a fork to the desired consistency.
5. Adjust the seasoning, top with lots of chopped fresh parsley and serve with freshly baked, crusty bread.

MAKES 250 ML (1 CUP)

Garlic 'Butter'

Excellent in garlic bread, this recipe is also delicious with the addition of finely chopped chillies, melted and poured over mealies or baby potatoes.

6 fat cloves garlic, peeled and chopped
60 ml (¼ cup) soya butter, softened
30 ml (2 Tbsp) olive oil
30 ml (2 Tbsp) chopped fresh parsley
2.5 ml (½ tsp) salt

1. Mix all the ingredients and use as required.

MAKES 80 ML (⅓ CUP)

Parsnip Purée

4–5 parsnips, peeled and chopped
1 x 400 g can butter beans
45 ml (3 Tbsp) olive oil
salt and black pepper to taste

1. Steam or boil the parsnips until tender, then purée in a blender with the remaining ingredients.
2. Adjust the seasoning and use as a dip or a spread on garlic toast or bruschetta.

MAKES 250 ML (1 CUP)

Roast Garlic

5–6 whole heads garlic
extra-virgin olive oil for drizzling

1. Preheat the oven to 220 °C.
2. Blanch the garlic in boiling water for 15 minutes. Drain and rub dry.
3. Place in a roasting pan, drizzle with olive oil and roast for 20 minutes until soft and easily squeezed out of the skin.

MAKES 30 ML (2 TBSP)

Mushroom Gravy

1 onion, peeled and diced
2 cloves garlic, peeled and chopped
30 ml (2 Tbsp) olive oil
250 ml (1 cup) mushrooms, washed and sliced
625 ml (2½ cups) vegetable stock
30 ml (2 Tbsp) soy sauce
60 ml (¼ cup) cake flour
5 ml (1 tsp) each of dried sage, thyme and marjoram
5 ml (1 tsp) herb salt
cracked black pepper to taste

1. Fry the onion and garlic in the oil until softened and translucent.
2. Add the mushrooms and sauté for 5 minutes over a high heat.
3. Reduce the heat and add the stock and soy sauce. Slowly stir in the flour, stirring well to combine and prevent lumps forming.
4. Bring to a simmer and then reduce the heat, stirring constantly.
5. Add the herbs, herb salt and pepper, and cook for 10 minutes or until thickened.

MAKES 375 ML (1½ CUPS)

Mushroom Gravy

Cajun Mustard

Cajun Mustard

250 ml (1 cup) dry white wine
5 ml (1 tsp) crushed garlic
5 ml (1 tsp) ground allspice
2.5 ml (½ tsp) salt
1 ml (¼ tsp) ground nutmeg
250 ml (1 cup) mustard seeds
60 ml (¼ cup) cider vinegar

1. Bring the wine, garlic, allspice, salt and nutmeg to the boil in a saucepan. Immediately reduce the heat and allow to simmer for 2–3 minutes.
2. Remove from the heat and set aside to cool, uncovered, for about 2 hours.
3. Lightly dry-fry the mustard seeds in a frying pan over a medium heat, and then coarsely crush them in a mortar and pestle.
4. Combine the crushed mustard seeds and vinegar in a bowl.
5. Put the saucepan back on the stove and bring to the boil over a high heat. Stir, then remove from the heat and add the mustard and vinegar mixture, whisking to combine.
6. Spoon into sterilised jars and store in a cool dark place. It will keep for 2–3 weeks, but refrigerate after opening.

MAKES 500 ML (2 CUPS)

Ginger Peanut Sauce

Delicious as a dip for crudités or as a sauce over noodles, this packs quite a punch with the addition of fresh chilli.
Kids love it, but if it's exclusively for them, you may want to leave out the chilli.

80 ml (⅓ cup) crunchy or smooth peanut butter
60 ml (¼ cup) water
30 ml (2 Tbsp) soy sauce
5 ml (1 tsp) cider vinegar
juice of 2 lemons
15 ml (1 Tbsp) grated fresh ginger
5 ml (1 tsp) sugar
5 ml (1 tsp) crushed garlic
½ red chilli, seeded and chopped (optional)

1. Combine all the ingredients in a blender and use as required.

MAKES 125 ML (½ CUP)

Store-cupboard Staples

More than just store-cupboard staples, these odds and ends are essential. What would you do without soup mix?

Or homemade, divinely delicious zesty salad dressing? Not to mention citrus salt, which can brighten up any dish.

Or pickles, comforting and homely on a huge wholewheat sandwich, dressed up with lettuce, tomato, cucumber

and a hearty dollop of mayonnaise … I digress, but I think you get the point.

Soup Mix

Use this soup mix in vegetable soups, such as the one on page 48.

250 ml (1 cup) barley
250 ml (1 cup) green split peas
250 ml (1 cup) yellow split peas
250 ml (1 cup) each of red and brown lentils

1. Pour all the ingredients into a sieve and shake well to get rid of any dust.
2. Store in an airtight container and use when needed.

Oven-dried Tomatoes

Delicious on sandwiches, in salads and over pasta.

2 kg medium tomatoes
10 ml (2 tsp) salt
30 ml (2 Tbsp) dried origanum or parsley
olive oil for sealing

1. Preheat the oven to 100 °C.
2. Wash, then top and tail the tomatoes, and cut in half horizontally.
3. Line a large baking tray with baking paper and sprinkle over half the salt and half the herbs. Place the tomatoes on the paper and sprinkle over the remaining salt and herbs.
4. Bake, opening the oven periodically to allow steam to escape. Turn the tomatoes after about 2 hours.
5. Prop the oven door open slightly and roast for another 2 hours, but keep an eye on the tomatoes – they reach a point where they burn fairly quickly.
6. Once dried out completely, allow to cool on a rack before putting into a sterilised, dry glass bottle. Top with olive oil to seal.

Salad Dressing

60 ml (¼ cup) sunflower oil
125 ml (½ cup) olive oil
60 ml (¼ cup) red grape vinegar
60 ml (¼ cup) lemon juice
60 ml (¼ cup) water
15 ml (1 Tbsp) Dijon mustard
5 ml (1 tsp) each of crushed garlic, fine salt, black pepper and dried mixed herbs

1. Whizz all the ingredients in a blender until smooth and creamy.
2. Allow to stand for about 1 hour before using. This will keep for 2–3 weeks, refrigerated.

Oven-dried Tomatoes

Lorne's Pickled Onions

Lorne's Pickled Onions

Store-bought pickled onions are all good and well, but to pickle your own onions gives an enormous sense of domestic satisfaction. Also, you can make them your way, with less or more sugar or spice and all things nice.

250 ml (1 cup) water
500 ml (2 cups) grape vinegar
15 ml (1 Tbsp) salt
15 ml (1 Tbsp) sugar (optional)*
5 ml (1 tsp) coriander seeds
5 ml (1 tsp) aniseeds
1 bay leaf
2 whole cloves garlic
3 whole chillies, tops cut off for the vinegar to infuse into the chilli
600 g small pickling onions

1. Bring the water, vinegar and salt to the boil in a large saucepan. Reduce the heat, add the sugar (if using), coriander seeds, aniseeds, bay leaf, garlic and chillies, and simmer for 10 minutes.
2. Meanwhile, peel the onions and place them into a sterilised jar. Pour the vinegar and spice mixture over the onions and seal the jar. Leave to cool and store for 2 weeks in a dark place.
3. Refrigerate once opened.

*Sugar is very often added to pickled onions. We prefer them unsweetened, but for those who like the sweeter taste, add sugar. Also, for less fiery onions, omit the chilli. By the same token, add more for a fierier batch.

Lemon Salt

This makes an excellent accompaniment to all veggies, especially roasted, and gives an added zing to popcorn.

500 ml (2 cups) fine sea salt
8 unwaxed lemons

1. Spread out the salt on a flat surface.
2. Firmly roll one lemon at a time in the salt, pressing down hard to release the oils.
3. Dust off the salt and set the lemons aside to use for lemonade (see page 140).
4. Ensure that the salt is completely dry before storing in an airtight container.

Note: The same principle applies to sugar; simply substitute castor sugar for the salt. Citrus sugar is delicious used in cake recipes or iced tea, or dusted over pancakes.

Home Herbalist

On offer to us is a bounty of indigenous plants and herbs, all of which benefit our health —

be it mind, body or spirit – in some way. South Africans have been making use of these jewels of nature

since time immemorial, and to tap into this pharmacopeia of 'restoratives' is as easy as investigating

what herb or spice deals best with specific ailments.

Aloe, for example, is one of our miracle healers, along with buchu and Devil's Claw. Bitter Aloe (Aloe ferox)

contains 34 amino acids, including seven of the eight recognised essential acids. Bitter Aloe is indigenous

to South Africa (mainly the Western and Eastern Cape, although a form of Bitter Aloe is common

to KwaZulu-Natal, between the Midlands and the Coast).

Soothing Skin Butter

Most well known for its laxative properties, aloe is also excellent as a treatment for arthritis, and the gel is widely used on open wounds as a healing salve. Freeze aloe gel in ice-cube trays, so that you always have a soothing balm for burns, bites or sunburn.

125 ml (½ cup) Aloe ferox gel
500 ml (2 cups) aqueous cream
2.5 ml (½ tsp) citric acid
20 drops essential oil of choice (I like acacia honey, but lavender is also nice)

1. Mix all the ingredients together for a soothing, moisturising body butter. For use as a sunburn treatment, keep refrigerated.

Note: Aloe has a carthartic nature and may stimulate uterine contractions and, in severe cases, cause miscarriage. Do not take internally if nursing, trying to conceive or pregnant.

Nappy Rash and Eczema Cream

Another of South Africa's wonder foods is rooibos tea. It has no side effects, is safe for people with kidney stones as it does not contain calcium oxalate, and is perfect as a night-cap as, unlike green and black tea, it does not contain any stimulants such as caffeine. It is packed full of antioxidants and it is now believed that it may help to prevent certain types of cancer.

45 ml (3 Tbsp) freshly brewed, strong rooibos tea
80 ml (⅓ cup) aqueous cream
10 drops citronella or lemongrass essential oil

1. Mix the ingredients and use as a soothing balm for skin ailments such as nappy rash, eczema and insect bites.

Bath Salts

Bath salts are easy to make and, once you have used this recipe, you may find that store-bought products aren't nearly as good as 'the real thing'! The ingredients are all natural and most people have them readily at hand. Who would have guessed at the healing properties lurking in the kitchen cupboard? Epsom salts have a soothing effect on tired aching muscles, while bicarb moisturises and softens the skin.

375 ml (1½ cups) coarse rock salt
250 ml (1 cup) Epsom salts
125 ml (½ cup) bicarbonate of soda
± 20 drops essential oil of choice

1. Mix all the ingredients and put them into an airtight glass jar.
2. Use 125 ml (½ cup) at a time.

Soothing Skin Butter

A Mindful Ginger Remedy

A Mindful Ginger Remedy

Ginger has anti-inflammatory properties, and alleviates the formation of inflammation on the brain. It also protects against free-radicals, which are a serious threat to brain health. Ginger is also an excellent way to ward off the winter chills. Here is a classic Hot Toddy recipe – just add a shot of brandy and you will sleep the sleep of the just.

45 ml (3 Tbsp) fresh chopped ginger
250 ml (1 cup) boiling water
5 ml (1 tsp) lemon juice
5 ml (1 tsp) sugar

1. Add the ginger to the water and allow to steep for 10 minutes.
2. Stir in the lemon juice and sugar, strain and sip slowly.

Aid for Arthritis

Devil's Claw, or Grapple Plant, is native to southern Africa and has been used for thousands of years as a treatment for the inflammation of joints, pain in the lower back and neck areas, pregnancy complications, and as a healing salve for open wounds. Today, Devil's Claw is used to treat degenerative joint diseases, and scientific study supports the use of this ancient remedy for the pain associated with arthritis.

5 ml (1 tsp) powdered dried Devil's Claw root
250 ml (1 cup) boiling water
10 ml (2 tsp) sugar (optional)

1. Steep the Devil's Claw in the water for 10–15 minutes.
2. Strain and add the sugar, if desired. Drink 1–3 times a day for back or neck pain and arthritic complaints.

Note: Devil's Claw is not suitable for consumption by small children.

Buchu Brandewyn

Another indigenous healer is buchu, used for centuries by local people for any number of ailments, including urinary-tract infection and gastro-intestinal illness. This herb has quite a heady 'shrubby' fragrance, and is commonly made into a tea, or into a compress by steeping the leaves in vinegar. Buchu is not suitable for pregnant women or small children.

3 x 5 cm-long fresh sprigs buchu
2.5 ml (½ tsp) ground aniseed
750 ml (3 cups) brandy

1. Steep the buchu sprigs and aniseed in the brandy in a jar, and shake well.
2. Store the mixture in a dark cupboard for 1–2 weeks, shaking now and again to infuse the flavours. Strain and drink (in small doses) to comfort a sore stomach, or before bed as a soothing sleeping aid.

Room Atomiser

Just about any essential oil or mixture of oils can be used effectively in this recipe. If, for example, you have a sick family member, spray a mixture of eucalyptus, citrus and lavender oil to refresh the room and dispel the 'vapours', an age-old remedy in a modern form.

375 ml (1½ cups) distilled water
15 ml (1 Tbsp) vodka
20–30 drops jasmine or lavender essential oil

1. Pour the water into a spray bottle or atomiser.
2. Stir the vodka and essential oils together, and add to the water. Shake well.
3. Spritz liberally all over your home for the soothing fragrance of summer.

Thyme Vinegar

An excellent traditional recipe for use in salad dressings, sauces and marinades, this is also an effective treatment for bites and stings, and can even be used as a sunblock!

500 ml (2 cups) white wine vinegar
60 ml (¼ cup) fresh thyme leaves

1. Heat the vinegar in a saucepan to just below boiling point.
2. Crush the thyme leaves in a mortar and pestle until well bruised and aromatic. Add to the vinegar and stir well.
3. Pour into an airtight jar and allow to steep for 2–3 weeks.
4. Strain and decant into a serving bottle.

Herbal Tea with a Slimming Twist

Because fennel is sometimes used as a diuretic, it can be useful as a slimming aid. It also eliminates toxins via the urine, and is wonderfully aromatic and fragrant, whether used in cooking, as a tea or as an infusion. The seeds also aid with indigestion and relieve hunger pangs.

5 ml (1 tsp) fennel seeds
5 ml (1 tsp) agave nectar (available at health and wellness shops)
250 ml (1 cup) boiling water

1. Stir the fennel seeds and nectar into the water and allow to steep for 5–10 minutes.
2. Drink while still hot, consuming 250 ml (1 cup) three times a day.

Index

Page numbers in bold indicate photographs.